Tales This Side
of the
Elysian Fields

Tales This Side
of the
Elysian Fields

Trevor W. Harrison

TALES THIS SIDE OF THE ELYSIAN FIELDS

Published by
Endless Sky Books
Regina, Saskatchewan, Canada
endless-sky-books.com

Print ISBN: 978-1-998273-24-9
Ebook ISBN: 978-1-998273-25-6

Cover painting
“Girl Sitting on a Rock” by Colleen Bakker

CONTENTS

"'Man was made for the earth.' Don't you think this eternal summer—these Elysian Fields—would pall upon you in course of time?"

—John Munro, *A Trip to Venus*

To

The Unforgotten

PREFACE

These stories do not an autobiography make. I generally like biographies, though not those okayed by the subject, but dislike most autobiographies for being self-serving and often boring. No one wants to be a prisoner condemned to listen to Uncle Bob repeat stories that lacked interest the first time around. The blessing of print and digital books is that readers can set them aside, something not easily done with Bob.

This collection of stories is culled from a briefcase—literally and figuratively—of memories. The connecting thread of each story is often travel. Each is presented more or less temporally, beginning with hitchhiking or driving across western Canada and the United States in the early 1970s and later travels in Europe and Asia in the mid-1970s and early 1980s. The stories are meant to stand on their own. Beyond travel, however, the centrepieces of each tale are the people, places, and events I encountered as a young man.

Though some of the stories we tell are outright fabrications, most are conveyed in good faith to others and, especially, to ourselves. They are approximations and interpretations; most often, justifications. Storytelling begins early on—"Johnny hit me; I didn't do anything"—and continues until our last breath.

Over time, our stories go through a kind of sorting house where the best ones are kept; some details foregrounded, others moved off-stage, a few shovelled into a cranial dumpster. Stories organize the bric-a-brac of our lives. They provide a falsely coherent meaning to things that may or may not have happened in a time and place that no longer exists. They impose an imaginary world of pretend linearity. Our stories are the offspring of a pleasurable intercourse between fiction and non-fiction, gestated over time.

The stories compiled here are from my "single" life, from my late teens and early twenties, ending a decade later. Most are based on notes taken at the time, only occasionally augmented by memory or Internet sources. With the exception of my family members and Dave, who features in "My Movie Career" and "Arab Work," the names of others and some locales have been changed.

Few things in life actually make for a good story—to anyone, that is, except Uncle Bob. My loyalty, first and foremost, is to the reader, so read and enjoy, and if you find this Bob-ish, move on.

NINETEEN: AN INTRODUCTION

The time between birth and nineteen is a kind of purgatory. One is not dead, but neither is one entirely alive; it's a kind of prep school for living. It has a Dickens-meets-Goldilocks feel; it is neither the best nor worst of times; sometimes fun and sometimes painful; warm, if one is lucky, as my early years were. The protective self is not yet formed; what exists is uncertain, wholly egoistic, often incompetent, and frequently capable of self-betrayal. But we stumble along anyway through the wasteland, grabbing what we think are life's lessons from burning bushes and much hotter places and desires until sometime after teenagehood, we leave home, never quite able to return.

My father, Gerald Keith Harrison, was of Irish and Scottish descent, mixed with a hint of Norwegian. Born in 1921, he was the youngest (by far) of seven children (one a half-brother), all but one of them boys. As a group, they were hardworking and hardliving, the Irish element ascendant.

My mother, Lena Alva Lindsay, was born in 1923 of solid Scottish and English stock, the second oldest of six children; also hardworking but with a tinge of Scottish Protestantism that mitigated against excess.

My parents grew up on farms mere miles apart in the Laurier district of western Manitoba. The Great Depression, occurring as they entered their teens, left scars—as it did upon the entire generation—that never fully healed, though stoically hidden from others. Like many people of that time, the Second World War ripped them away from what a scribe once described as "the idiocy of rural life."

I was born in 1952, seven years after the war had ended, yet—like many of my confreres—I was a child of that war. Films, documentaries, the news: everything reminded us of the recent cataclysm that effortlessly rolled over into the Cold War. Both my parents served in the actual war. My father saw the world courtesy of the 18th Manitoba Dragoons. He was a radio operator whose task was to ride out to the front line in a staghound and do reconnaissance. He landed on Juno Beach mere weeks after D-Day, in time to witness both the horrors of war and the joy of Holland's liberation.

My mother was spared the war's material scars but felt them nonetheless, serving in Ottawa's wartime administration, where she honed skills that later proved highly useful in civilian life. No one really escaped the war.

Keith and Lena married in 1946 and soon settled in Winnipeg's St. Vital district. Two years later, they welcomed a son, Marvin. My father cut ice blocks out of the Assiniboine River for use in ice machines, a bloody cold job, while my mother worked as an office accountant for a small business, a job only slightly warmer in its intent.

But in 1950, the Red River flooded, as it is wont to do, taking out their rented home. My parents moved to Edmonton without me but welcomed me when I was born two years later. Alberta was then in the midst of an oil boom, one of many rollercoaster rides in the years that followed that always saw the petro-rug pulled out from under prosperity. My family's first years were spent in a rented apartment just off Jasper Avenue. Later, we moved—renting again—to a wartime house south of the university.

A mildly Dickensian story. Up to the age of six, I was a free-range mongrel, riding a bike, shooting passersby with my Roy Rogers guns, or playing the heroic role of Zorro, though—due to an absence of black fabric—the cape my mother made for me was red. Suddenly, however, as I was turning six, I was dispatched to something called "a school." Its locale was a large, red-brick Edwardian—that is, industrial-looking—building just south of the University of Alberta proper. None too creatively, it was called "University School." Later renamed Corbett Hall, it later became a teaching facility for nurses. In the 1950s, however, it was a Normal School; even more, it was the province's most illustrious institution for teacher training. It was there I attended Grade 1 in 1958, of which I have three distinct memories.

The first memory is of my first day of school, sitting at a desk, crying inconsolably at my loss of freedom. There was scarcely anyone in the classroom whom I could shoot or run my sword through.

My second memory is of the school's principal, a gaunt and austere man who, in keeping with the times and his position, invariably wore a grey or tan suit. His primary role, at least as he saw it, was to instill discipline, often by way of a hard and ridged leather strap, with which I soon became closely acquainted. Upon the first offence, a student received a warning; upon the second offence, the strap was administered once to each hand. Thereafter, according to a precise geometric calculus, an escalating number of welt-raising assaults was delivered: two, four, eight, sixteen, etc.

I don't remember the precise number of floggings each of my hands received, though it was at least eight. I do recall, however, some of the charges on my rap sheet. On one occasion, I was wrestling with some fellow six-year-old ruffians in a park near the school, ignoring the commands of a crossing guard. On another occasion, I absentmindedly doodled on a clean blackboard, using coloured chalk, while the class waited in line to go somewhere. For this venal sin, I was sent to the office for instruction. Flinching one's hand at the moment of being strapped was another offence, punishable by additional strappings—an act that earned me further demerits.

My third and much more pleasant memory of Grade 1 is Beth. Beth was my first, though not my last, love. She sat three chairs up in the row to my right. She seemed very shy and sweet, my attraction to her amplified by her flowery, even sensual, pastel dresses. One day, however, some unchivalrous student pointed out that beneath her chair a small pool of liquid had formed. Embarrassed, Beth lowered her head onto the desk and cried. I felt bad for her, but the magic was gone; fickle me.

The family moved that year to a freshly minted home, no longer rented, in the newly birthed suburb of Ottewell, formerly the sprawling farmland of a family by the same name. Our house was the second built across what was then a major road, 75th Street. The undeveloped land behind our home was a treasure trove of fascinating and dangerous objects—rusted horseshoes, old and bent license plates, railway spikes—which my brother and I, and our cocker spaniel, Star, duly exhumed on regular walks searching for the nests of the elusive prairie chicken.

Ottewell was a working-class neighbourhood with a smattering of professionals. In later years, it produced—by my count —a prominent doctor, a police officer, a professor of physics, a union organizer, a nationally known artist, and a nurse who volunteered overseas. Not bad.

My new school was Holyrood Elementary, which had gained a new principal that year. As luck would have it, he was my old nemesis from University School. But the move seemed to have leavened both our personalities. We started our relationship afresh; I was not strapped that year nor in any year afterward. I changed schools again the next year; and the next, the result of endless rezoning. My early years were thus spent as a kind of itinerant elementary student.

I remember fondly several of my elementary teachers: a woman who cried in telling the story on Remembrance Day of her brother who had died during the war; a young bespectacled man who shared his egg sandwich the day mine fell apart on a school outing, and who another day brought to class a mosaic tile portrait of Cleopatra he was making; another female teacher who, impressed with my drawings in Grade 4, offered to pay for my art lessons (my parents declined); and another male teacher who in a Grade 5 science class posed the unanswerable but intriguing question of what was outside of and contained our known universe?

When not in school, my brother and I played long, sweaty games of table hockey, for which I made a schedule of regular season games between the six original NHL teams. I kept a record of the scores and individual statistics for goals and assists by all the positions. I even awarded at season's end imaginary trophies to the most deserving teams and metal-bound players. I liked stats.

I also liked wars. When not playing table hockey, I assembled a large army of military toys, playing with such intensity and realism that the parents of a neighbour boy finally forbid him from playing with me.

In evenings, our family played cards—poker, bridge, cribbage, rummy—or board games (*Monopoly* or *Sorry!*) or watched one of the two available television stations, whose offerings plumbed the entire catalogue of film back to the 1930s. Our home sported a number of books with photos of far-away peoples and places, of ancient buildings and landscapes, and history, but especially atlases, which I poured over endlessly. Machu Picchu, Niagara Falls, the Parthenon, the Pyramid of Cheops, the Rock of Gibraltar, and the Taj Mahal were as familiar to me from early on as were the aqua-coloured dinner plates and bowls set on our kitchen table.

Nonfiction—Churchill, Gibbons, Shirer, and Wells—held equal status on our bookshelves with poetry and fiction—Bronte, Shakespeare, Tennyson, and Wells again. My knowledge of literature was burnished by *Classics Illustrated Comics*, which my mother happily bought for my brother and me. I remember distinctly, too, the day in 1962 when the volumes of the *Encyclopedia Britannica* arrived, each page an invitation to mysterious places, things, and people.

But my interests ran decidedly to world history and geography. Baudelaire once described a malady, a horror of home. I did not suffer in horror, but the books, maps, and photos did awaken a longing to be somewhere—anywhere—else.

To these stimuli was added an eclectic array of music played on our large console stereo. My parents, but especially my father, loved music, everything from operatic tenors to orchestral suites, from country to pop and gospel, from classical guitarists to jazz trumpeters. On any given day, Beniamino Gigli might sing a prelude to Nat King Cole; Mahalia Jackson to Marty Robbins; Andreas Segovia might play an introduction to Al Hirt or Rimsky-Korsakov; and later, of course, The Beatles.

Our summers away from school meant more time to wander the neighbourhood or play indoor games. My parents bought an undeveloped property fronting Pigeon Lake, south of Edmonton. It was one of the very few large bodies of water in Alberta where bloodsuckers and noxious weeds did not lie in wait. In the early years, we spent many weekends clearing brush, cutting down trees, sleeping in a burlap tent, swimming, and cooking on open fires. We had a flotilla of lake-worthy vessels that included a small rowboat, an oil-barrel raft, and—eventually—a varnished canoe of craftsman-like quality. As time went on, the property took on the appearance of a quaint Appalachian shantytown, occupied by a small trailer and an assortment of metal sheds and wooden shacks, including a two-seater outhouse. Only much later, sadly after my father had passed away, was a proper cabin built.

Every few years, our family drove across Saskatchewan to western Manitoba to visit uncles, aunts, and cousins in the small town of McCreary or my maternal grandparents in the larger and picturesque town of Neepawa.* Before settling into town life—an older two-storey home, veranda in front—they had farmed outside McCreary; before that, my grandfather was a professional photographer of some renown. Now, they supplemented their income with boarders, with whom, in awkward silence, we ate our meals.

Two other memories. The first: my grandfather giving me a deactivated First World War grenade, a treasured prize. The second: his funeral four years later, in the course of which my grandmother gave me some licorice, black and brittle like old electric cord, contained in one of his suit pockets, inedible. Strange the things that sequester in memory.

The prairie roads and cars of the time made each vacation an adventure. Endless construction, detours aplenty; overheated car engines, blown timing chains, broken alternators, or torn generator belts; uncomfortable sleeps in a cold car waiting for gas stations to open; and car radios blaring Buck Owens or fire-and-brimstone preachers warning of Satan. But it was all worth it because waiting at the end were my country cousins, all of whom seemed to live a curiously exotic life in comparison with my mundane Big City existence.

Ours was a typical working-class family. My mother, by virtue of administrative skills learned during the war, became supervisor of the University Hospital's night admitting staff, while my father first managed and later owned an autobody repair shop. My brother and I rarely visited our mother's place of work. My memories of the hospital are vague: white walls and labyrinthine tunnels that ran beneath the hospital's hulking superstructure.

I do have one very precise memory of it, however.

---

* Margaret Laurence is buried there, despite the fact that some townsfolk apparently didn't like her, displeased by what she wrote about them.

I woke one morning when I was eight years old with my left testicle very red, very large, and very painful. I was rushed to the hospital, where surgeons quickly diagnosed my case as a testicular torsion and as quickly operated to save my exploding ball and, indeed, my life. Bedded next to me in a hospital room was a young boy crippled by polio. I've often wondered what happened to him.

I remained in hospital for several days, becoming quite adept at racing my wheelchair up and down corridors. Days later, after my release, I awoke at home to find my right testicle similarly swollen to the size of a large, ripe nectarine. Once again, I was rushed to hospital; more days in a ward, more wheelchair racing. I was told later that my surgical daily double would likely put me in a medical book, a rather dubious fame. But the incident was not without reward as I had extracted from my mother a promise—if I lived—to get a cat.

Bursting testicles aside, my father's body shop held far more interest than the hospital. It lay in the heart of what had once been Edmonton's garment manufacturing district, but which by the 1950s was the city's decaying inner city, "a locale synonymous with both personal and civic failure," as I later wrote.[*]

The shop was the repository of an alien world: strange tools —car jacks, welders, and assorted hammers, covered in grease and grime and strewn about the floor or hung from walls; the sweet smells of oil[†], turpentine, thinners, and paints, at a time before people much considered the danger of such fumes; and the cacophonous sounds of machines mixed with the shouts of blue-collar workers, four-letter words and broken English dancing on the air, strange and exotic to my young ears.

The streets outside the body shop were an equally strange

---

[*]   Trevor W. Harrison, Trevor, *Prairie Bohemian: Frank Gay's Life in Music*. Edmonton: University of Alberta Press, p. 35. The book provides additional descriptions of the shop and surrounding area.

[†]   A section of the building housing the shop was leased to a business specializing in the recycling of old oil, an enterprise well ahead of its time.

and colourful mix of people and sights, with hints of danger, pathos, and excitement. The area's immediate focal points were the King Eddie and Royal hotels, where Dad sometimes took my brother and me for burgers and (Hires) root beer. Every booth had a jukebox where you could plug in a quarter and listen to Johnny Horton or Johnny Cash.

Today, fear stalks many urban landscapes. But then, Marvin and I rode buses unaccompanied from the south side to downtown, going to movies at the Gem, the Paramount, and Capitol theatres or shopping at the Bay and Eaton's stores. Until the 1970s, the majestic MacDonald Hotel was still the tallest building on Edmonton's horizon. On the street corner across from it, an older gentleman, wearing a long, dark, formless coat invariably stood, day after day, holding out to passersby a small pamphlet while asking in a truncated Eastern European accent, "Do you want to have a testimony of what Jesus did?"

In his forties, having thus far dodged the serious injuries that await blue-collar workers and also wanting a different challenge, my father decided to complete his high school and go on to university. His enthusiasm for learning was contagious, especially as related to courses he took in English and anthropology. He would return nightly from classes telling us about Chaucer, Ben Johnston, and Alexander Pope or Richard and Mary Leakey and the sharpness of obsidian blades; a description made real when he showed us his freshly shaved forearm, courtesy of the instructor's hands-on teaching.

It was an exciting, if scary, time to grow up. The nightly television, newspapers, and radio featured a parade of wars, assassinations, sex, space rockets, and amazing music, chaperoned by the omnipresent threat of nuclear annihilation. (And in Canada, the FLQ Crisis.) The world beat a path to everyone's door, should they care to open it, much as today's youth are the inevitable products of 9/11, Middle East wars, the Russia-Ukraine war, recessions, the Internet, and environmental collapse. We are all products of our time.

Grade 10 saw me attend what was then Bonnie Doon High School in Edmonton, later renamed the Vimy Ridge Academy. I made the mistake in literature class of telling the teacher that I didn't think Shakespeare's *Twelfth Night* was very funny, that it was actually rather boring. She berated me for what she said was my imperious tone and called me "Little Caesar." The nickname stuck with me the rest of the year.

More valuable to me in the long run was the typing class to which I was assigned as part of a group of students placed in the business stream. The class was made up overwhelmingly of young women, being prepared for a future life as secretaries if not stay-at-home moms. The few boys in the class, including myself, were there presumably because we seemed neither suitable for the trades nor for the academy, neither fish nor fowl, as it were. The teacher was twenty-something, a slim and pretty recent graduate, a fact which ensured the near-perfect attendance of male students. However, my training on the typewriter's anachronistic keyboard proved invaluable as the world moved into the computer age.

My father dodged another fate around this same time in the

form of a congenital heart defect that required surgery, a not inconsequential thing at the time (or even now). But he, and the family, persevered, and, in time, he was ordained a minister. My father was inspired by ideas of social justice, based on civic morality rather than religion *per se.* My mother's beliefs were rooted in a sense of kindness to others, though these had a veneer of doctrinal, if sometimes confused, religiosity. Both were members of the United Church, whose Sunday services, as a wag famously remarked, were the New Democrats in caucus.

He was ordained in 1968. The headline of an *Edmonton Journal* article preciously read that he had gone from restoring (auto) bodies to healing souls. No less than in any profession, ministers must pay their dues. And so, when he was ordained, my father was assigned a charge in a small Central Alberta town, where he also provided services to some even smaller hamlets. We moved to the main town, where—in compensation for a relatively meagre salary—the family was provided a manse in which to live.

The move was difficult for all of us. My father's chief burden was knowing the strain the move placed on the rest of the family. My mother's burden was to give up her hospital administrator career, though—true to her nature—she made the best of it, cultivating new friends and taking on volunteer work in the community, while still longing for a return to full-time work. My brother, who had recently finished high school, lingered at home. But I was going into Grade 11 and mourned the loss of friends and familiarity, and the chance perhaps to continue playing organized football, while also hating my new role—that of the minister's son—for which I had not auditioned and which I viewed as a permanent and impenetrable barrier to meeting friends, especially teenage girls. The song "Son of a Preacher Man" had only just been released and struck me as wholly overblown in its optimism.

And so, shortly after we moved into the manse, I did what every angry, acne-faced, alienated, and horny teenage son of a

Protestant minister does: I decorated every wall of my down-stairs bedroom with my vast collection of Playboy and Pent-house centrefolds, to that point carefully secreted in a Kodak X-ray box. I then invited my parents into my room to survey my new wallpaper. To their credit, they did not yell; in fact, they barely said anything, though my mother, in her usual restrained manner, did opine that one of the girls—her name was DeDe Lind—was "pretty."

The road to "me" opened.

I never felt at home in the town and made no lasting—and few temporary—friendships. I didn't dislike my new fellow students, and don't think they disliked me, but we didn't know each other and had no time in which to bridge the yawning gap. In the end, the move was the best thing that could have happened to me. It tore me away from Edmonton, from old ties and previous identities; it freed me.

At the time, however, any benefits seemed illusory. My already marked indifference to school soared. My school grades, barely treading water, descended into new and wretched depths. My high school math teacher (also the school principal), a warm and kindly man of the Mormon faith, noted on one report card that I "wandered the Elysian fields." I slept little, staying up all night reading novels and writing bad poetry, but mostly thinking of far-away places and more distant girls. I wanted nothing so much as to leave home, to physically wander, to go—somewhere. It was with great relief—for myself and perhaps the school—when I exited high school, sans a diploma, in the spring of 1970.

The family moved again that year, to a town close to Edmon-ton. I took a correspondence course—chemistry—with the aim of bolstering my diploma credits, but indifference again won out. I enrolled in a broadcasting course where I learned the word "often" must be said with a silent "t." Futility, with a loud "f," scored a gold medal.

At nineteen, the world and time stretch out before you. You can't wait to escape your life, the one that is trapping you. You are enthralled and captivated by an invisible world, so close you can almost touch it, but which quickly vanishes. You want to rush toward it, through it, but you don't know what "it" is. The past is gone; the present a burden; the future scary, yet everything.

All I knew—though it was more a feeling than an articulated thought—was that the three most important things in my life were women, travel, and writing; but I was still a shy virgin, had not yet travelled outside—and not much within—Canada, and could provide no evidence suggestive of literary talent. Thus, standing solidly on thin air, I left, never again to fully experience the warm clutches of home.

My real life began.

~

*M*any compatriots of my age will relate to the stories told here; stories of working, travelling—when it was much safer than today—and generally growing up, in the West at least, when the Age of Aquarius was ascendant. The next three stories ("My Railroad Career," "In Praise of Dumbass Jobs," and "California Dreaming") are an homage to jobs I held after high school and travel to California in the early seventies. The next four stories ("Gran Canaria," "Incident in a Small Village," "Barcelona, Con-Men, and Bulls," and "Paradise Lost") arise out of a trip of five months I made in 1973 to Europe and the countries of the southern Mediterranean when I was twenty. The next two ("Near Death by Rabbit" and "The New Orleans Blues") are largely tales of hitchhiking in North America, a common phenomenon of the 1970s.

By 1976, I was pounding the keys of an old Underwood typewriter, was no longer a virgin, and had held for the first time a real job—one with a purpose beyond a paycheque. The two stories that follow ("My Movie Career" and "Arab Work") arise out of an overland journey to India in 1976, an experience recounted more fully in a book, *Safarnameh**, but absent these two stories. The final four stories ("A Horse Dies in Kashmir," "Travels in Ladakh," "Srinigar and the *HMS Kipling*," and "Dalhousie, Dharamsala, and McLeod Ganj") relate experiences and observations from a trip to northwest India in 1983.

---

* *Safarnameh: A Travellers Journey Along the Hippie Trail*. Forthcoming, Athabasca University Press, Spring 2025.

MY RAILWAY CAREER

Dauphin, Manitoba, early October 1971. I stepped over the steel rails and walked toward the Canadian National Railway roundhouse. Its sepia brick frontage was faded and lifeless beneath a foggy streetlight. Back of the roundhouse, a giant grain elevator loomed. A half-moon stared out from a curtain of cloud, a scene from some grainy silent film. A drenching rain slopped down from the dread sky.

Days earlier, the railway company had hired me to work on an extra gang, defined as a crew of blue-collar workers who do maintenance on a stretch of railroad track. Today, I was reporting to CN's Dauphin office in preparation for travel somewhere the next morning to work at something. The job paid little more than minimum wage plus meals; still, a fair return for a nineteen-year-old unsuccessfully discharged from high school. Besides, having already decided to one day be a successful writer, I considered the meagre pay the price of a real-life blue-collar experience, the sort of thing about which Faulkner would have written.

I approached the roundhouse. A big, hard-bitten man in blue dungarees stepped out of the shadows. "The foreman and time-keeper are not 'ere," he said with a Ukrainian accent. Confusion.

"To tellink you da troot," he continued. "You should 'ave come aarlier," he added, dragging out a hard R. He said I should return the next morning.

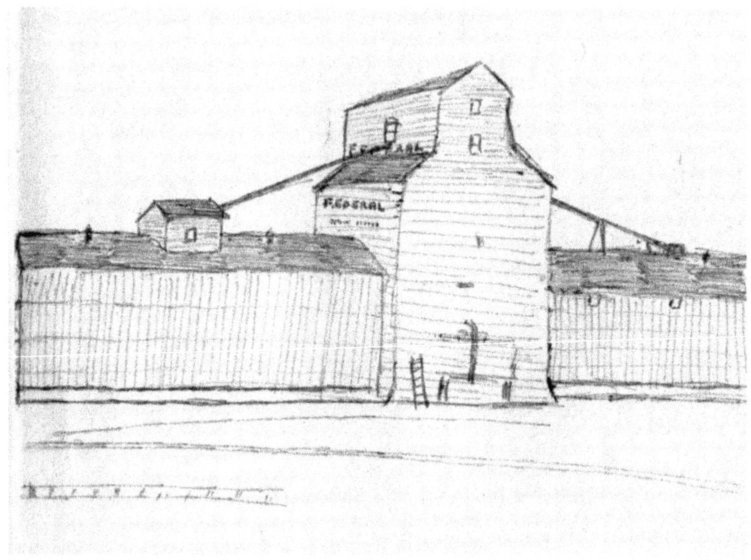

And so, I did. A different older man, even less talkative, led me to a bunk car. I sat the next few hours on a bed in an unlit car, occasionally getting up to open the door and stare into the silence. Then, a man I later learned was the assistant foreman arrived. He reeked of booze. Like others who followed, he looked like a character from a 1940s Hollywood C movie: the nervous, shifty-eyed thug. The thug looked at me and growled, "Well, I didn't know nothin' about this since you got no papers." More confusion, mixed with annoyance, mapped his face, compounded by something else. "I just finished one helluva fuckin' night on the fuckin' town," he said. "All I can tell you is put your name, address, and social security number on a fuckin' piece of paper. I can't promise anything, though." A difficult search produced a pen but no regular paper. He handed me a paper towel. I scribbled my information on it.

All was made right, however, when, a while later, the foreman arrived. The parade of Hollywood characters continued: Joe Friday, trying to find his way back to the Naked City, speaking little, wanting only the facts. Evidently, my facts were enough. I was hired.

Now securely employed, I looked around my quarters. The bunk car's green walls were bare, except for some crude, felt-pen drawings of naked women with helpful arrows pointing to their vaginas and a few crude anatomical labels. Written on one of the bunkhouse doors were the words "Yesterday's Mansion"; on another, "Fred's House."

My bed, like the rest, was thin and dirty, its mattress set over a simple metal frame. It was covered with two sheets and an equal set of coarse woollen blankets. A small coal-oil stove dominated the centre of the bunk car.

It was a cold fall day, but the car was hot and humid. A million flies swarmed. Rain buffeted the car's walls, and with each blast of wind, it swayed. A small, snaking river of rainwater slithered from under the doors. At intervals, when the storm abated, I opened one door to broom the water out.

I looked around the car again. A shelf displayed a strangely literate array of books: Costain's *The Magnificent Century*, Hardy's *Far from the Madding Crowd*, Crane's *The Red Badge of Courage*, Fischer's *Gandhi*, Steinbeck's *East of Eden*, and Hope's *The Prisoner of Zenda*. I thought, *Surely, these are not the books of the old man, the drunken assistant foreman I met earlier, or the artist whose works decorate the walls?*

The day dragged on. I wondered when we were leaving—*if* we were leaving. The rain finally ceased. I wandered over to a store and bought a copy of *Catcher in the Rye* that I spotted languishing on a shelf. I got supper at the nearby Greyhound station, then sat on the stoop of the CNR office reading. Tired but engrossed in the book and lost in the growing haziness of evening, I looked up and, for a moment, imagined the train—my train—pulling out. I bolted from the stoop, running toward the train, before realizing that another train was shunting past:

Einstein's relativity at work. I returned to the step. Just then, a railway guard came by.

"You think this is a library or somethin'?" he barked.

"Why?" I replied, genuinely dim to his sarcasm.

"Whatya doin' here?"

"I'm a railroad worker, section gang," I stumbled, then suddenly remembered a number the foreman had mentioned. "Gang member, ah, one-forty; section one-forty."

My fumbled utterance worked. Frozen before my use of the secret code, his demeanour abruptly changed. "Okay," he said. "It's just there's a lot of weird people around here."

The day wore on. I returned to the bunk car to a sleep born two-thirds of boredom and only one-third of fatigue. A while later, a jolt; I felt the car shunt, heard the train whistle blare and its wheels squeal. 7:30 p.m.: we were moving.

Lulled by the sound and rhythm of movement, I fell asleep. Then it stopped. I kept sleeping. Just after midnight, I awoke to a sudden noise. I had thought the car's doors were locked. Now, standing in the car, looming over me and staring, was the "tellink da troot" man, larger than ever. He was babbling fast and furious and shaking and waving his hands, a human windmill. Propped on the bed by an elbow, bleary-eyed, I watched him wordlessly for a couple of minutes, then calmly told him, "I don't know what you're saying." He continued to ramble on for a while, then left. Shortly, the train began moving again. I fell back asleep.

I was in Kamsack, Saskatchewan, when I woke the next morning. The town's population today is less than 2,000. It was no more in 1971.

The bunk car was cold. I left it and went for a walk around 9:30 a.m. to warm up. The town was clean and empty on a Sunday. Kamsack was a typical prairie town in late rigor mortis. I found a small café; actually, the only one. A television screen was showing an NFL game, San Francisco and Philadelphia. I sat in a booth watching the game, ordering repeated refills of Hires root beer, killing time, and then returned to the bunk car. Later that evening, the car began its final journey to Corcoran*, Saskatchewan, a town not much larger than Kamsack, roughly thirty-eight kilometres away.

~

I slept through the night, waking the next morning to the noisy arrival of my bunkmates. The older Ukrainian had travelled in one of the railcars. Mysteriously appearing were the foreman and his assistant, someone titled a "C-class engineer," and a cook, along with his assistant. Two young labourers in their mid-twenties arrived in a red Dodge Charger. They sported buzzcuts and carried their cigarettes rolled up in the upper sleeves of their t-shirts. Two other young workers—Laurel (skinny) and Hardy (slightly overweight)— drove up in a Comet. They were students on a gap year, making money for university. Like me, they had shoulder-length hair, earning the foreman's labelling of us as hippies.

Then there were George and Lennie. George, clean-shaven, tall and lanky, was in his late thirties. He was, I soon learned, the custodian of the classic literature I had seen earlier. At first meeting, he seemed the epitome of the lean, rugged cowboy, the Garry Cooper type, replete with a clipped, taciturn manner of speaking. I learned later, however, that his gaunt frame was the result of a crippling bout of ulcers, made worse by chain smoking. But George had also suffered several personal hardships, including the death of a child. Still, he never complained; just went about his work. Most of the time, he looked at the rest of us like a thoughtful, if bemused, father. When he spoke, the others listened. He was the crew's unappointed foreman and Lennie's unspoken guardian.

Lennie needed a guardian. He was a short, stumpy man who lived with his elderly parents in another small Saskatchewan

---

* The town's name has been changed.

town. I thought at first that he was in his fifties, but in fact, he had barely breached thirty. The chief cause of this fraud was his thin, white hair, brushed from left to right, which sat like a late-fall wheat field flattened by prairie winds. He moved and thought slowly, awkwardly, and without awareness. His speech was sometimes given to vulgar slurs and wild vagaries. At such moments, George's hand might come to rest invisibly on Lennie's shoulder, his silent voice saying, "Calm down, Lennie, it's okay," steadying Lenny's lurching ship and steering him away from hidden shoals.

The bunk car had fairly basic sleeping arrangements. A brace of very small single beds occupied both sides of the car. Each was provided with cold white sheets and coarse blankets that felt like steel wool ripping your flesh. There was a sink with hand soap. Warm water was provided every morning via a pitcher and basin. Portable outhouses awaited outside.

The cookhouse occupied a separate car. The head cook was a stalky man in his fifties with false teeth that slopped about in his mouth when he spoke like a bobbing raft at sea. His hair was thinning, and his nose had the blistered, rosy look of an alcoholic, which he was. He never looked directly at anyone, taking a furtive glance only. He constantly wrung his hands as though trying to get clean. The hours between meals saw him cradling a bottle of Five Star. Each afternoon, he ambled past us, heading to the town's liquor store.

The crew took the cook's drinking in wary stride as they did the knowledge that the assistant cook was—in the slur common to the times—"a faggot." This information was conveyed as neither a warning nor a joke but rather as a fact, like ice being cold.

Workday began at 7 a.m. with a hearty breakfast in a mess car: thick pork chops and long slabs of bacon, slathered and swimming in their own fat, surrounded by islands of broiling eggs; hash browns; vats of porridge; towers of toast, regular or French; pancakes, sentries of butter, jam, and pitchers of corn syrup standing guard; and metal carafes of warm coffee, cream at the ready. Quantity there was, but of quality much less. By a remarkable feat of culinary skill, the cook and his assistant succeeded in levelling the cumulative taste of everything to something akin to salted or sugared Gyprock. But eat we did, returning, again and again, to fill our plates, sitting only long enough to scarf down the food amid mumbled conversations before heading briefly to our bunks to wash up and comb our hair.

By 8 a.m. we were at work, or rather standing in the vicinity of work, such opening forays beginning with slow talk, the lighting of cigarettes, and a marked lack of enthusiasm for the day ahead. But soon enough, noon would come, and with it lunch, another hefty dose of protein, fat, and sugary carbohydrates, then back to work at 1:30. At 5 p.m., we returned to the cook house: more carbohydrates, but mainly cold sausages, pork chops, and potatoes left over from earlier. We would then retire to our bunks to clean up and sometimes wander into Corcoran, but only for a time as the town offered little by way of stimulation. Fall was now fully upon us; the sun set sooner each day. We collapsed in our bunks. I remember the fatigue my body felt each night. It was a good tired, the kind that, when you're young and male, tells you with every movement that you are a man, seeming to float above the earth, above even time and space: immortal.

~

*W*ork on an extra gang is hard and, although simple, nonetheless involves a degree of skill. Depending on the job, one might use a variety of tools, including hand tampers, picks, shovels, saws, and rail tongs— but mostly hands. The work is mind-numbing, which also makes it dangerous. A CN job posting describes extra gang workers as continuously "waiting to start work while performing various tasks." Waiting was itself chief among these various tasks.

Sleep-deprived from travelling, I spent my first day of work in a daze, unhearing and unthinking while endlessly pulling out railway ties. On later days, my work consisted of lifting or replacing wooden railway ties and tie plates and levelling and tamping the ground beneath the ties. Part of each day involved throwing the fresh plates from a flatbed car, which had arrived with us, onto the ground, where other workers carried them down the line to be used.

The tie plates were jagged, rusting, and always cold, becoming worse as fall took hold. Each morning, a glint of frost dusted the plate like icing sugar. Though we wore leather gloves, the plate edges caught with every toss, ripping through the fingers and stinging. We changed gloves at least once, sometimes twice, a day, though never into new gloves, only other, less-used older ones, hoping they were better than the discarded ones. In time, my fingers grew calloused but still sported red pinpricks of blood. I returned each night to the bunkhouse with swollen fingers.

My fourth day of work saw us whipped by fall winds, reaching a hundred kilometres per hour. I spent the afternoon levelling the ground around the track. The foreman came by and advised me quietly not to dig holes too deep. No sooner had he left than the C-class engineer came by. He noted the steel-toed leather boots I had bought for the job.

"What did you buy those boots for?" he barked. "Dig, don't scoop! Like this." He took the shovel from my hand and proceeded to show me how to dig a hole, ending with the imperious command, "Use those boots, mister!"

The moment of insult—of emasculation—did not end there, however. No sooner had the engineer departed than the assistant foreman showed up. He was heartily disliked by all for his drinking and belligerency and had been fired once before, an outcome the crew hoped would soon be repeated.

"No, no! Use the shovel like this," he declaimed. Like the engineer, he took my shovel—by now, I was feeling quite possessive—and showed me how to quickly "scoop" the ground around the ties, an action not unlike that for which I had been corrected only minutes earlier.

Such were the workdays: fatigue, sweat, and boredom, the minutes broken by occasional harangues from Oberleutnants-in-training. More often, however, we talked about hockey or, in the case of the two buzzcut young men, tales of their recent successes with women and the number of beers drunk the previous weekend.

Corcoran ensured there was no life outside of work. The town's main street—its only real street—was a hundred yards across from the rail cars and work site. The street featured a bar and pool hall, next door to which was a café. The rest of the street was fleshed out by squat and dilapidated homes, hovered over by pine and willow trees. Prairie grass and weeds grew high along the intersecting gutter. When we arrived in early fall, grasshoppers still flitted about the grass, but they were soon gone with the onset of winter. The skies were now grey—solemn rather than foreboding.

The Thanksgiving break being long enough, most of the crew went home—or to whatever constituted home. I rode with Laurel and Hardy to Saskatoon and a weekend of pub crawling, concluding at the famous Palliser hotel; then we headed back to Corcoran. But such escapes were rare and only reinforced the work's monotonous ennui.

Bunk car evenings sometimes saw a poker game. As some participants played better than others, there could be angry losers, but as the games were penny-ante, there wasn't enough to fight about. On most nights, however, we were too tired to do much other than read books and magazines or write letters home.

One evening, a few of us, including George, Lennie, and I, went into town, hitting the bar and pool hall. We had the premises pretty much to ourselves and sat at a table that soon sported bottles of Canadian or Blue, but George drank only water—his ulcers. He watched the others, saying little, as usual. His guard dropped for a moment as he told us he had once been in the military, rising briefly to the rank of lance-corporal before running into trouble with a major. Then silence.

Lennie sat to my right, fondling a beer bottle and then several, engaged in his own conversation. His eyes wandered.

He asked George and me if we saw "those women" sitting over there.

We didn't.

He told us they were spreading their legs and showing him their . . . well . . . gynecological parts, though his term would not be one used in *The Lancet*.

Quite definitely, we didn't see this either. George and I looked away and returned to our conversation. A while later, we headed back to the bunk car. The next day, Lennie missed work.

"I don't think he's going to last another two weeks," said George. I didn't say anything but wondered how long I, too, would last.

A few days later, I was again tamping the ground. George, who was the unofficial leader of our small group, said we needed another tamping machine and told me to go down the line and get one. I hadn't headed far before a familiar voice sounded. It was the assistant foreman, who handed me a shovel.

"Here, take this! Don't stand around like a lost sheep!"

One cold morning soon after, I rose from my hard bunk bed. Stiff of muscle, my calloused hands still throbbing, I sought out the foreman. He was just settling into breakfast, cutting into some eggs and bacon strips. I told him I was quitting. His face was more expressionless than ever. He mumbled something about my final cheque being mailed.

I walked slowly away in my fancy steel boots past my now former workmates. They were busy, waiting for work to begin, lighting cigarettes, talking of the night before and of nothing. I glanced at the vanishing world of the extra gang and felt at the moment strangely guilty, as though I was letting my fellows down. A short chorus of shouts and harangues rose from the other assembled men. (Did I imagine George looking at me, not speaking, but issuing a glancing wave?)

I crossed the rail line, pack slung over my back, over the tracks into town. The dry prairie grass was thigh-deep, its ripe summer sheen giving way now to a spindly yellow. A grey mist hovered above the rooftops. I walked to the town's outskirts and stuck out my thumb.

The sky's fat belly opened up, spilling cold rain over the slick, black, quiet, and lonely highway. Cars, blind and oblivious, rambled past for seeming hours, splashing. I stood invisible in the pitch daylight, the water squelching between my toes while thunder belched, and lightning flashed. My feet grew numb, and my shivering teeth vibrated like a rivet gun. I lit a cigarette.

A farm truck slowed. "Where ya' goin'?" asked the driver.

"Home," I said.

"Where's that?"

"I don't know."

"I can take you to Togo," he replied.

I got in and didn't look back; the last spike in my railroad career.

IN PRAISE OF DUMBASS JOBS

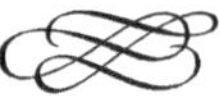

On either side of my railroad career, I worked at a series of what are best described as dumbass jobs. They are the staple of employment for someone just out of high school. Someone getting a dumbass job is fortunate, but only if the job doesn't lead to permanence. The road to hell is paved by good pay and stability.

To be clear, dumbass jobs are not the same as bullshit jobs. As described by the late David Graeber, bullshit jobs are meaningless and unfulfilling. Examples include consultants, communications coordinators, and corporate lawyers. So employed, they go each day to work at something they hate doing in return for a high salary, good benefits, and wholly unearned prestige.

Dumbass jobs exhibit no such golden shackles. While often more socially useful than bullshit jobs, dumbass jobs pay much less and lack status. The benefit package includes free, if cold, coffee. Mothers rarely boast to friends that their sons and daughters have embarked on careers in dumbass jobs.

Dumbass jobs require minimal skill, a level of ability most young people are able to achieve. The jobs are monotonous and boring, though sometimes dangerous, the latter actually mitigating to a degree the tedium. Together, these things make leaving dumbass jobs easy.

I worked at several dumbass jobs early on; let me count the ways.

When I was nineteen, I worked a few months in Edmonton's Eaton's store in what was known as its "white goods department." White goods meant kitchen items such as fridges, stoves, and freezers. The term "white" referred to the fact that colour had not yet been invented.

My job was to take delivery orders from floor salesmen—always men—who had convinced a customer—nearly always a woman—to buy a certain appliance. I was to move the said item to a large, industrial elevator, where it could begin its journey to a home in the suburbs.

Like the railroad job, the job appealed to my young, male sense of muscular identity. It didn't require a huge amount of thought. There was minimal paperwork—perhaps my signature on a shipping document. (Paper versus electronic documentation is a clear dividing line today between dumbass and bullshit jobs.) It required only strength, the agility to avoid crushing my hand or foot, and the ability to calculate the most efficient way of fitting appliances into the elevator. It was like an early form of Tetris, but with bigger blocks. For a reason I never quite understood, I was instructed that the elevator never travel partially filled. It was to be lowered only at day's end, stuffed to its arterial walls, to the shipping dock below, where delivery trucks awaited.

I enjoyed the people I worked with—the salesmen, the secretaries, and my two coworkers (a young man and woman who lived together in a loft and were often stoned)—but grew bored after a few months. The frenzied whip of tedium drove me on to another dumbass job.

Some years later, I worked in a Bay sporting goods department. My tasks involved re-folding polo shirts and re-boxing shoes disturbed by customers. One day, an irate customer came in demanding his money back for a set of deadly lawn darts that he said were broken. A careful forensic examination showed they had been chewed flightless by a huge mastiff. No matter: the customer is always right. He got his money.

My only claim to knowledge of sporting goods was that I could throw a football (well) and hit a golf ball (not so well). I had, however, recently bought Nike running shoes, which were then new on the market. When customers sought advice on cross-trainers, I could proudly point to my feet. "Great shoes," I'd say. I made Nike what it is today.

Somewhere along my work trajectory, I trained to sell Britannica encyclopedias. I was joined by four other trainees, two women and two men. We met in a small office building rented by the company. If successful in our training, we were promised a future of back-breaking work for minimal pay and no benefits, relying on commission sales to pay the rent.

Our instructors were two well-dressed company representatives, one man, one woman. Over three days, we learned the sales "script," a pitch whose every word and phrase, tone and rhythm, had been laboratory tested for its precise impact. Our task, before being released into the world, was to memorize each line and to say each word with the proper level of clarity, emphasis, and enthusiasm. The script included embedded moments of jovial humour designed to build a convivial rapport with the prospective buyer. The entire presentation lasted perhaps ten minutes, with pauses for breath. It was a stage performance of low quality. It was not a Shakespearean soliloquy.

Within minutes, I determined the job to be of the dumbass variety, made worse by the robotic demands of the script. I have often wondered since whether stage actors sometimes fight an urge to break rank and do the unexpected. ("Not this time, Brutus!" Caesar grabs the knife and runs his assailant through.)

On the last day of training, the five of us performed our role before our instructors. By secret ballot, the trainees were to vote for the winner, who would receive ten dollars. One of the other trainees was a young man who, like me, looked like a rejected member of a Jesus cult. It was clear that the winner would be either him or me as neither of us stumbled over the words, and both snickered appropriately, but subtly, at our well-rehearsed quips. The vote was held. I lost three votes to two to my hirsute companion.

As we left the building for the last time, knowing that neither of us was going to sign on for the job, we talked about it, the acting, and the vote. Fool that I was, I had voted for him. He confessed he had voted for himself. We went off for a beer. He paid. I remembered the script for years afterwards, a reminder of one dumbass job narrowly escaped.

I was also a car jockey for a time when I was nineteen. The term "car jockey" falls under the wider umbrella of parking attendant. Parking attendants inspect, clean, and maintain vehicles, sometimes picking up and dropping off customers and returning vehicles to them. A subset of attendants are valets, those who rush up to greet you at swank hotels, pleasant of smile and open of palm.

I had the status of neither a parking attendant nor a valet. My initial work site was the head office of a car dealership. My tasks were few: vacuum out vehicles, scrub and polish their interiors and exteriors, clean off snow. If necessary, move them around the lot, into the wash area, or into the showroom.

The first of these tasks was easily achieved. Handling a vacuum, hose, or chamois cloth is not a job requiring years of preparation. Driving, however, presented something of a problem, as I had not yet got my licence. And, while I knew how to drive, or at least how to start a vehicle, I wasn't legally supposed to be doing it. For this reason, I was soon demoted to the dealership's farm club, a small secondary office that dealt only in used vehicles.

The four or five salespeople there were middle-aged men. Many were divorced. Some were entering, others leaving, the AA door. Most had been car salesmen for several years and had done the tour of dealerships. I was shown on my first day at work a collection of grungy coffee mugs, each with a distinguishing logo or personal name. A salesman told me—an evidently long-standing joke—"The mugs change, but the cups remain the same."

Conversations were marked by a good-natured joviality awaiting the arrival of customers. On cold days, when no one came, talk centred on stories in the local newspaper. The sudden arrival of a prospective customer was a blessed event. The sauntering of a live body onto the lot, even if by accident, caused a stir, followed by discussion about whether they looked like real customers or just "tire-kickers." An overt, if silent, air of competitiveness hung over the small office, encouraged by a posted scorecard, revised weekly, that tracked who was at the top for sales.

The office was cramped and either hot or cold. My tasks were minimal, my enthusiasm for the job even less. On most days, I had to fight the urge to sleep. I was a bad car jockey and soon quit the job.

At some point after, I took on a temporary job at Edmonton's Masonic Temple. The temple still stands, though its classical lines are less imposing, dwarfed by the city's modern skyline. Like the Masonic Order itself, it is part of a vanishing world.

I worked there for three months as a janitor, filling in for the position's vacationing long-time occupant. To this day, I'm not sure how I got the job, as neither of my parents were Freemasons nor belonged to any of the animal orders—Moose, Elk, Lions, or otherwise—who roamed Edmonton's urban jungle.

A good janitor views the building he is caring for as his home. A good janitor is constantly looking for things that need cleaning or repair. It is hard work. I was a temporary replacement, however, and in any case, the temple was not my home. It was a job for which I was being paid minimum wage, nothing more.

The temple featured a large, central gym. Among my major tasks was ensuring it was kept clean and the wooden floor polished. But as this did not occupy much time, on other days, a large bolt of keys in hand, I wandered the temple halls and visited its many break-out rooms. Inside many were impressive wooden pews and chairs with carved inscriptions and long desks. The panelled walls featured similar carved figures. I was reminded of the British courtrooms I had seen on television. But there were other rooms for which I had no keys. The locked rooms, along with a *Book of Rosicrucian* I found one day languishing in a cupboard, added to a welcome sense that I was in the presence of a mysterious secret cult.

Most of the time, however, I hung out in a small cloakroom just off the gym, wondering what else I should be doing. Thinking of nothing, I sat there, daydreaming and reading or writing notes. I had a thin book of Robbie Burns's poetry and tried to write pieces mimicking the sound and cadence of his verse. My efforts were bad, even for doggerel, with lots of "e'res" and "e'ens," but it occupied my time until five o'clock came around.

The most demanding element of my work was preparing for gatherings of the Minus One Club. It was a group of people, generally over fifty-five, who had lost a partner through death, divorce, or desertion—hence its name. They met once a month on a Friday evening, for which I was required to work late. It was my job to set up card tables and folding chairs along the walls of the gym, the inner quadrant being reserved for dancing to recorded music. I greeted the attendees as they arrived, dutifully hanging their coats in the cloakroom and giving them a numbered claim slip in return. Teenage girls hired for that evening brought up food prepared in a basement kitchen. The guests purchased wine from me—red, white, and rosé—which I brought to their tables. It was my job to ensure the guests were happy and that the wine kept flowing.

The event usually shut down around midnight, at which point I would hand the members their coats, then do a preliminary clean up before taking down and putting away the tables and chairs. Sometimes, I augmented my meagre wages by consolidating the wine left in assorted bottles into one that I would take home.

One warm evening during my second month of employment, a gentleman strolled out onto the front stoop to have a smoke and talk with friends. A moment later, he collapsed—a heart attack.

Hours earlier, he had been dressing in his finest for the evening. Minutes before, he had been dancing, quaffing back a glass of cheap rosé, perhaps chatting up a woman as lonely as he in hopes of taking her home. Now, he was laid out on the Masonic Temple's steps. I had seen dead people before, but no one who died suddenly. His face had not yet drained of colour.

A small crowd had gathered on the steps, which were bathed now by light from the temple's window and the glow of street-lamps. Someone felt the fallen man's pulse. He confirmed the man was dead. "He was just talking, then . . . ," said a man.

"I think he was dead before he hit the ground," said another.

The first man nodded.

To one side, a woman in a saffron dress averted her face, tucking it deep into the collar of her pink jacket. A delicate carnation was stapled to its lapel. She sobbed quietly. Was she the one he had been chatting to? Should the police or an ambulance be called? No one seemed quite sure.

A Minus One attendee re-entered the temple. He went to the cloakroom office, where the desk phone was located, and made calls to both. No one was sure if he should be moved inside, so we just stood around and waited until an ambulance arrived.

Several weeks later, the club held another dance. The evening progressed much as planned. No one died. But dumbass jobs don't always go smoothly. At the end of the evening, as everyone gathered their garments, a patron, a Friday regular, stepped forward and handed me his claim stub. I checked the rack, then checked again. "The grey one," he said. I checked a third time for his long, grey coat. No amount of searching sufficed. I realized with some horror that minutes earlier I had given a similar grey coat to another person. (Dumbass jobs have a way of making you do dumbass things.) My error was a bad thing, made worse by the fact the coat contained his car keys.

The patron was very drunk and very belligerent. I tried to convince him that, because of his condition, it was perhaps a good thing that he did not have his keys. This rationale escaped him. At length, and with many apologies and the help of more sober attendees, I settled him. I took down his address and phone number and assured him that his keys and coat would no doubt be found and soon returned to him by another attendee who would realize the error.

It was at the moment of writing the enraged patron's name that I recognized him as one of the salesmen at the car dealership where I had previously worked.

That's one of the things about dumbass jobs. Unless you escape them altogether, they keep bringing you back to the same place. Still, they are invaluable when you're young. They teach you how to deal with a lot of types of people, good, bad, and in-between. They leave you with lots of stories to tell at parties. They tell you about yourself. Most importantly, they convince you that you don't want to be working at dumbass jobs for the rest of your life.

Eventually, I moved from dumbass jobs into a series of jobs that I like to think were not bullshit jobs. None of them bored me and made me wish I was somewhere else. In each case, they allowed me to think creatively and to continue meeting interesting people. To a degree, I now think the work I did made a positive difference, though probably not as much as I thought at the time.

Another story.

CALIFORNIA DREAMING

*U*ntil recently, winters in western Canada in January have been cold. The year 1972 was no exception. And so, Robert, a childhood friend, and I planned our escape to California. And why not? We were in our late teens, jobless, and free. We knew nothing of California except what we'd learned from Beach Boys songs and television. But how difficult could it be to get there?

Armed with bravery borne of naivety but little money and dressed in the *de rigueur* uniform of the day—faded jeans, t-shirts, and khaki jackets bought at an Army Surplus store, backpacks slung over our shoulders—we set off into the unknown. For Robert, the trip was primarily a search for sun. For me, however, the journey was, from the onset, cast in the sepia overtones of a Jack Kerouac adventure.

We travelled by Canadian National train from Edmonton to Vancouver. The ticket cost $20. We arrived tired the next day and checked into the nearby, rundown, and squalid Ivanhoe Hotel. Built in the early twentieth century, today it is a backpacker's hostel, though with some long-term accommodations and a ground-floor pub. During its years between birth and resurrection, however, the hotel was a skid-row flop house, cheap accommodation its sole attraction.

Some adventures are planned; many are the product of luck; some are the result of stupidity. Our first adventure took the latter form.

Google reliably informs me the distance from Vancouver to the border post at Blaine, Washington, is a little over fifty kilometres. We arrived at the crossing by bus late in the evening. It was dark. Backpacks in place, we walked, silent and tired, toward the customs station.

And kept walking. Robert had left Canada before but only in the company of his parents and I not at all. This being long before 9/11, COVID-19, or Donald Trump, the border was seamless to our tired eyes. Neither soldiers nor lights nor the sound of trumpets heralded our arrival.

Two blocks farther on, however, the border achieved material status when an American border patrol car drove up, lights flashing and sirens blaring. Two officers got out.

"Where ya' goin'?" asked one.

"The bus station," I replied.

"I mean, destination?"

"California."

"Why didn't you stop at customs?"

This was clearly a question of some import, to which neither Robert nor I had a good answer. "Get in the car, boys," said the officer, whose badge read RENE. We drove to the deportation office.

"How long will this take?" I naively asked. "We have a bus at 8:13."

"You don't have to worry about that, boys," said Officer Rene. "You're under arrest."

At the office, the questioning continued.

"What grade did you guys finish?"

"Twelve," we said, oblivious to the sarcasm.

"And you didn't know you had to report to customs?"

We were fingerprinted and photographed. Could a prison cell be next? No. Instead, we were driven back to the border and told firmly to enter the United States properly next time.

We walked back to White Rock, roughly six kilometres from the US border, and waited outside a train station until dawn's early light. Posted on a wall was a train schedule. Behind a wicket, an older woman was beginning her workday.

"When's the next train?" I asked.

"Hasn't been a train here in six months," she replied. I wondered if I should tell her that she could go home now. She pointed us in the direction of the bus depot.

Bus tickets soon in hand, we again crossed the border. A guard asked where we were going and why. He liked our answers. Soon, we were on our way to Portland.

~

The Portland bus-stop cafeteria was plastered with signs. One warned us it was illegal to purchase cigarettes if underage. A second informed us that "*Playboy* and *Penthouse* are available under the counter." (Remember, this was 1972.) A third sign, above a pinball machine, its knobs furiously beaten by a desperate man, read, "It is unlawful for anyone under the age of 21 to operate these machines, under City Ordinance X"—this, I thought, when American soldiers of eighteen were still dying in Vietnam and would continue to do so for the next three years.

I poured an instant coffee and thumbed through small packets, looking for cream. A pigeon-eyed matron watched from her perch behind the cash register.

"That's more coffee," she deadtoned as my fingers fumbled a Nescafe packet. "Read the signs, please," emphasis added. Yes, more signs.

"Can I order toast?" I asked. *Toast is cheap*, I thought. We were already on a tight budget, hoping our meagre funds would get us through until the Canadian winter had shed its skin and we could return.

"Only what's on the menu, sir." Toast was not served.

Our bus started up again. Robert and I re-embarked for the ride of more than eighteen hours through Salem, Medford, Sacramento, and more obscure places. We passed at first skiffs of snow, iron-red hills, shale and sand, then scant green fields and cauliflower-like trees, until at last we were in San Francisco. It was 10:45 p.m. as the bus pulled into the downtown station on Turk Street in the city's Tenderloin District. Because we knew nothing of the city, it could have been a station anywhere. We stood in the breathing darkness, unsure what to do next.

A thin, young African American dressed in a long coat walked out of a movie scene toward us.

"Got a watch?" he asked.

"No."

"Want one?" he said and opened his long, grey coat to display his many wares.

"No, thanks," we said. He walked away.

We checked into the nearby YMCA, where we claimed—not entirely a falsehood—that we had no money. This led to a visit from a gentleman known as "the night minister." He was, literally, a man of the cloth, whose role was to deal with transients. He cheerlessly grilled Robert and me for an hour about our circumstances and had us fill out paperwork. At last, we were provided a room for the night, another experience achieved.

The next morning, after leaving our packs at the bus station, we set off for Golden Gate Park. We played football with some kids and then headed back to Market Street. We had survived the last twenty-four hours on bus-stop coffee and junk food and were very hungry.

Robert and I had been friends for several years. I knew him to be conservative and conventional by nature; pushing the envelope of experience was not his forte. Having already embarrassed him by way of the night minister episode, I now re-doubled his discomfort by convincing him that we should go to a Salvation Army for lunch.

San Francisco has a temperate climate. The morning was still cool but warmed up quickly as we strolled along, I in front, Robert a few yards behind. Suddenly, a thin and scraggly young man in jeans ran toward us. He was followed by someone shouting incomprehensibly. The first runner had already passed me when I realized the second was a policeman. "Stop that man! Stop that man!" Too late for me, but Robert—who was bigger than me—instinctively grabbed the young man's arm, enough to spin him off balance. He stumbled a few feet, then fell. The policeman and several bystanders pinned him to the ground.

"You stopped that guy!" I said in something approximating awe. Robert shrugged. We kept walking.

I asked a man on the street where the Sally Ann was. "Up there," he pointed, "two-and-a-half blocks. I'm going there myself." We followed and soon arrived.

Several men of various ages milled about in front of the headquarters, most sporting long hair, beards, and shabby clothes. One man was telling the others how he had learned to roll cigarettes in prison. Another individual stood conspicuously removed from the others. Perhaps in his mid-twenties and clean-cut and wearing a long, grey coat, he stared out from his personal foxhole with slitty, tearful eyes. With mouth open and teeth bared, he talked aloud—but not to us—in slurred utterances or sometimes emitted animal sounds. He was accompanied by an unseen companion, Godfrey. "Is that you, Godfrey? Jesus Christ saves." He laughed. "What d'ya think of that, Godfrey?"

The doors to the Sally Ann opened. Godfrey's companion slipped from view. The rest of us shuffled into the building. We had dues to pay before eating, however. We watched a film about the immorality of war, then went into a large mess hall arrayed with long, wooden tables, before which were communal benches. We sat beside our fellows. A bowl of warm and hearty soup was brought, along with stale, hard bread—all of this washed down with black coffee.

We left the Sally Ann, another experience notched, but agreed we were still hungry. We headed toward a hotdog stand passed earlier. Across the street, several cop cars suddenly squealed to a halt. A half-dozen police officers poured out of them. The police quickly pinned a white male to a wall while freeing a girl from his clutches.

"Good! They got the bastard," a nearby drunk intoned. "I saw him beatin' a girl in the alley, kickin' her."

We began walking again. As we went, street pedlars sitting on blankets greeted us, offering to sell us cameras, watches, beads, pot, and mescaline. But we had no money and weren't into drugs. Besides, our minds were set on a hotdog.

We stayed that night and the next in a hotel near the YMCA. We paid $5.26 per night. Two days later, we began hitchhiking to San Diego.

~

The Pacific Coast Highway from San Francisco to San Diego is a little over an eight-hour drive, but hitchhiking is a different matter. Being at the whim of luck and strangers much can go wrong. We didn't have a map, only a vague direction: south. The rides we flagged down took us along desultory paths that, on the first evening, led us inland to a wayward gas station in Fresno, where we ended up sleeping in a derelict car whose door was open. At night, the desert sheds its warmth, and this was winter. White frost hugged the car's cold metal. The vehicle offered no break from the cold, so we shivered sleepless until morning. Then, we began thumbing again.

A single male hitchhiking may catch a ride. A male and a female are even more likely to find success. But two young males hitchhiking could wait a long time—unless, as it turned out, they were wearing army jackets.

An older gentleman in a nice, new vehicle pulled over. Before many words were exchanged, we got in.

"Where you boys heading?" he asked.

"San Diego," we said.

"You boys on leave?"

It was now clear. This was 1972, and the Vietnam War was still being fought and still a point of polarization between hawks and doves. Our driver, evidently a hawk, believed we were members of the US military, probably soldiers back on R&R. When he realized we were two clueless teenagers from Canada —perhaps even hippies—the conversation came to an abrupt halt. Still, he was polite and civil. He drove us to the outskirts of Los Angeles where, from a truck stop perched high above, we saw briefly the shining city lights and then caught another ride. Some hours later, our feet graced San Diego's asphalt streets and briny shores for the first time.

We wandered about for a few hours but stumbled at last upon an old white-washed two-storey adobe-styled hotel a few hundred yards from the Pacific Ocean. The ancient San Juan Hotel had once been rundown but was now several steps below that level. But it was cheap—US$100 a month—and fit our budget and that of the hotel's permanent residents, a host of aging and unwell pensioners. Everything about the hotel, including its residents, had the feeling of decay and imminent death.

Our room was about ten by twelve feet, with a single queen-sized bed and a small night table and chair. Attached to the room was a small, dirty bathroom with a shower. There was a tiny communal kitchen inside the hotel that had a fridge where residents kept their food, carefully labelled as to ownership.

The hotel manager was Arnold, a man of perhaps sixty years whose responses, depending on what he was asked and when, ranged from minor grumbling to slightly audible anger. He told us he went to bed every evening at precisely 8 p.m. We suffered his wrath once when we woke him at ten to ask for toilet paper and towels, which the caretaker—an overweight and sparsely toothed but friendly woman—had inadvertently forgotten that day to supply. He was not pleased. Posted prominently throughout the hotel were Arnold's Commandments:

"Thou shalt not use kitchen after ten."

"Thou shalt not have a hot plate in your room."

"Thou shalt not play a radio loudly after ten."

"Thou shalt not have a bicycle in the hotel lobby."

Strewn about the hotel's premises were copies of these rules, ripped up by incensed—or perhaps just mischievous—residents. Arnold dutifully replaced the edicts every week.

The other residents were friendly; many were old and frail.

The maintenance man, who was married to the woman caretaker, had a receding chin and dull, blank eyes. He moved slowly, though not in any methodical way, and spoke in a monotone voice.

A tiny, elderly woman lived down the hall. Every day, whether rain or shine, she polished her car, a vintage 1950s model, rarely driven. She sometimes complained to me about the noise made by the other residents. She thought Robert and I were nice boys but also considered us strange and secretive because we often slept in late and spent so little time in the hotel. It was then that I learned she and the other residents believed—as did the driver who had picked us up hitchhiking—that we were soldiers on leave, perhaps suffering from post-traumatic stress.

The hotel was a kind of retirement home for the poor. "You know, I'm paying three times what I paid at the other place," she told me, adding, "and it was nicer, with a private bath. Seventy-five dollars a month, and I only paid twenty-five at the other place." She then paused. "Of course, that was thirty years ago!"

In our time there, the San Juan Hotel proved to be a very leaky vessel. The bathroom sink's rusted pipes dripped relentlessly. Every morning, we woke to the pipe's rhythmic drip, the water slowly filling the waste basket we had set beneath. One day, the maintenance man came to "put washers on," followed the next day by yet more washers, and the next day, too, to no avail. The drip continued, an annoying though harmless form of water torture.

One evening, while I was reading and the maintenance man was fitting more washers, his wife shuffled in, wearing her large, rainbow housecoat and fluff-floppy slippers.

"There's a fight goin' on out back," she announced. "I knew there was goin' to be a fight tonight. I could hear them swearing up and down the alley. Mother this, and mother that." She laughed and left the room. Her husband finished his work again.

"See you tomorrow," I said.

But our water problems had just begun. One night, while Robert and I lay on the bed, contemplating sleep, a spew of water gushed from the overhead light fixture, followed immediately by a "pop" as the electricity shorted and the bulbs burst. We dashed from the room and sought out the manager, who, as usual, was sound asleep and none too pleased to see us. The cause of the leak was soon found: the similarly faulty bathroom pipes in the room above had sprung their own leak. The water was soon turned off, and we went back to our darkened room and the dampened sheets. Fresh bedding arrived the next morning, along with the maintenance man, who restored the light and began again the Sisyphean task of installing new washers.

~

*B*eing short of cash, most of San Diego's excitements were beyond our reach. One day, though, we scrounged up money to ride a huge but lonely Ferris wheel, from the top of which we could view the sprawling city's expanse. Another time, we snuck into a posh hotel off the ocean and swam in their pool for a few minutes before being discovered and unceremoniously escorted off the premises. But most of the time we just aimlessly wandered the city's busy streets or walked the sandy beach, listening to the Pacific waves and enjoying the warm weather, thoughts of Canadian snow banished. The fact is, in the later words of Gord Downey, we were looking for a place to happen, which, in the unspectacular fashion of our actual lives, was not much.

Penury ruled. Every dollar not wasted meant another day in the California sun. So, we ate breakfasts and lunches at McDonald's, where burgers were nineteen cents and fries and root beer likewise cheap. Once a week, we walked to a restaurant some miles away named Georges that featured a smorgasbord. In the manner of teenage boys, we stuffed ourselves outrageously on pork chops, chicken, potatoes, and lots of sweets—forget the salads—and would leave George's with doggy bags. Sugar donuts filled our stomachs between meals.

And we went to movies. I remember, in particular, *El Topo*, today described by Wikipedia* as a "1970 Mexican acid Western film . . . characterized by bizarre characters and occurrences, use of maimed and dwarf performers, and heavy doses of Christian symbolism and Eastern philosophy." Being unsophisticated teenagers from Canada, Robert and I thought the film weird and boring. Much more to our liking was the second film on the double-bill, *The Omega Man*, starring Charlton Heston as the survivor of a global pandemic, a theme of recurrent interest, as it turns out.

We reprised our movie night a while later, this time seeing Walter Matthau in *Kotch* and a romantic comedy, *Lovers and Other Strangers*. The shows ran late; unfortunately, our bus did not. It was a long way back to the San Juan, but we decided to walk, following a service road that abutted the freeway. At one point, the road veered sharply away so that we couldn't follow the freeway any longer and hopped a fence onto the freeway. Our intent was to similarly hop the fence on the other side and so follow the freeway home. Doing so was, of course, illegal and dangerous. Barely had we stepped onto the freeway, just beneath

---

* https://en.wikipedia.org/wiki/El_Topo

an overpass, when a police car drove up, sirens loud and lights burning. All I could make out were two figures silhouetted against the lights.

A police officer jumped out of the car. "Get out some identification," he said, followed by, "Put your hands in the air." I could see the glint of his gun against the car lights. His partner, Officer Two, who had been the driver, stood beside him, mute.

I had not then heard the phrase "Catch-22," but this was surely it. I lowered my arms slightly in an attempt to get my ID.

Officer One repeated, "Keep those hands up." I again reached for the sky while Officer Two frisked both of us. He felt something in my breast-coat pockets.

"What are those?" he asked.

"Cigars," I replied. They were, in fact, cigarillos, but this did not seem the time to offer distinctions.

"Both pockets?"

"Yeah."

More frisking. Slowly, heedful of being unthreatening, we pulled out our wallets. The officer looked at the information and quickly concluded, much as had the border police at Blaine, that he was dealing not with dangerous felons but with two very stupid kids from the frozen north. "Okay, boys, into the car."

So, for the second time, we rode in an American police vehicle. We were given a court summons for a couple of weeks hence and informed that failure to appear was punishable by arrest should we be found otherwise in the country. In retrospect, I don't remember being scared, though I was very careful in lowering my hands. But I also wonder now, years later, what might have happened had I been black? How we come to experience our experiences is not always clear at the moment.

Our fingerprints were already on file from the border incident; we didn't want to add to our rap sheet by failing to appear in court. So, a couple of weeks later, we went to the designated courthouse and sat on benches beside other miscreants charged with an array of penny-ante offences. Another experience.

Robert was again embarrassed, but I watched with interest each trivial case that came before the judge as though I were at a Broadway play. No murders, no assaults, no major robberies, just misdemeanours, but real stories nonetheless. At last, our time in the dock arrived. We told the bored judge our story. It had no complicated plot, so it ended quickly. We pleaded guilty, paid our fine, and made our way slowly out of the courthouse.

By then, our California adventure was coming to an end. We had been in the US for six weeks and were nearly out of money. It was time to go home. No hitchhiking this time; we bought tickets on a bus from San Diego to Vancouver and from there to Edmonton. I had all of twenty-five cents in my pocket when I opened the door to my parents' home. I owed Robert a pack of cigarettes.

It was late February; Canada was still cold.

GRAN CANARIA

The year was 1973; the place somewhere on the Atlantic Ocean, just off North Africa. The ocean waves licked the floating underbelly of Tenerife's volcano. A pod of dolphins escorted our ship while seagulls, tucked in behind, poached Atlantic fish thrown up in the wake. It was our fourth day out from Algeciras, still hours and miles from our destination; yet there it was, the largest of the Canary Islands, until suddenly—as Donovan Leach wrote, "First there is a mountain, then there is no mountain"—it was gone.

The mirage was an unplanned gift. So, also, was the voyage, in this case, bestowed by the American state department. Until days before, I was bound to Morocco, Marrakesh, Casablanca, and Rick's café. But the US government, with its usual respect for other jurisdictions, pressured Morocco's government to make it difficult for Western youth to enter the land of kif. So, at twenty years old, on my first travel outside of North America, and without reason to do otherwise, I changed plans. The Canary Islands were my default, though by no means a poor second.

Being single and confined to a ship for four days, one inevitably joins a tribe of fellow passengers, and so it was with me. There were seven of us, all Canadians, bound culturally by hockey, the Guess Who, and English—nary a francophone Quebecois among us. Cole was a pencil-thin and practised young doper from smalltown Ontario. Terry (or Terrence) was a dedicated cynic—Toronto will do that to you—who, though only in his late twenties, was already scouring the bottom of liquor bottles for life's purpose. Gordon was a lonely bullyboy from a small logging town in British Columbia. He missed his boozing buddies and mistakenly thought his tales of drinking exploits would impress Tracy and Jane, two Twiggy-like high school friends from Regina who were on a gap-year adventure before settling down to whatever young Prairie girls settled down to at the time. Finally, Rob was a burly lobster fisherman from Halifax who looked pub-brawl dangerous but was quiet and, as the Spanish said, "*muy tranquilo.*"

Were it not for being at sea together, we might all have swum in different waters. But bonded anew by Spanish-infused penury, we together rented a penthouse apartment in Las Palmas. The word "penthouse" hints at a wholly underserved note of luxury. Save for being on the top floor, the set of rooms and appointments was spare and uninspiring; the furniture was basic, the beds hard, the sheets long past their prime, and the cooking utensils and cutlery unworthy of theft. Nonetheless, it was a place to stay for a couple of weeks.

It was early spring. Each day, the clouds rolled in off the Atlantic and roiled against the gun-metal sky. We would saunter, beer in hand, to a small, enclosed beach nearby to imbibe the sun's rays and body surf. The latter activity involved heedlessly propelling one's body into the six-foot Atlantic waves, from whence one was thrown, turning and twisting, onto the gravelly shore, where fine pebbly stones were stapled into our chests: the absurd and abandoned joys of youth. Most of the time, however, we did nothing, which in one's late teens and early twenties constitutes pretty much everything. Wedged between activities of meaningless importance, we carried on self-indulgent and angst-driven conversations while drinking Cuba Libres and absinthe; absinthe, presumably, makes the heart grow fonder.

Returning to the apartment one evening, I noted we had been joined by Irene and Patty, two Americans in their late twenties who lived in a separate apartment and a man in his mid-thirties with thick, dark, twisted hair. He sported a tweed jacket, an open-collar shirt, and new jeans. He looked the epitome of a university professor, which indeed he was, the type of unkempt professor you might even find in an English department, of which, again, he was.

Jacob was, as I quickly learned, a Jewish-American professor of English at a California university. Though only in his early thirties, he had already written three books and was on his way to a moderately successful academic career. I had never met a real author before. I was smitten.

We sat on the floor and talked around a rectangular table. Scattered across the table were empty wine and beer bottles, some glasses, paper cups, matches, and rolling papers. Earlier that day, Cole had scored some hash and most of us had by now indulged, with Cole and Gordon quaffing the lion's share. I was only mildly impaired, fatigue the main impediment to my focus. The collective smoke had rasped my throat so that I didn't much feel like talking, content instead to watch the unfolding scene. Rob, more engaged than usual, carried a hash pipe around the room, offering to be a good host, blowing smoke up everyone's nostrils. He came to our author-guest, who politely declined.

"I don't smoke. I get high from words, from people," he said and began asking Irene what had brought her to the Canaries. His comments about himself were perfunctory, even disinterested. He was serious, and seriously respectful and attentive—more than I think was warranted—to the pot-induced twaddle of a lot of twenty-year-old kids. I wondered later if he might have been doing the James Michener research thing ("What does the average male/female, twenty-something, middle class, person do/say/think/feel?" etc.) But, no, I think he was just genuinely interested in us. We were not mere specimens.

I continued to say little. It was not just the hash. Over the past few days, I had heard much of what everyone else had to tell of their lives. It wasn't especially engaging the first time, and certainly not the second and now third.

For the author, however, it was the first time, and he wanted more. Unfortunately, hash smokers are generally poor conversationalists. Outside of a few scatological offerings, they tend to eat and fall into a slow stupor. Jacob was undeterred, however. He decided to force a conversation.

He began telling folk tales, acting out a variety of characters. The group at first laughed, but with each set, became more uneasy and unsure. Then he broke into reciting Dylan Thomas, replete with the roll of a Welsh tongue.

"Have you ever heard his recordings?" he asked. "Fantastic voice."

I was pretty sure no one else in our group had ever heard of Bob Dylan's namesake. No one answered. The stoned troupe was fading into the cheap woodwork. While our author's energy threw sparks, our assemblage retreated further into darkness. The atmosphere became discordant.

Cole, who had bought the hash and smoked by far his due, became edgy. "Are you trying to teach us something? Is that why you're here?"

"No," said our guest. "I was invited to crash the night. What could I teach you? What are you afraid of?"

Cole continued to ask if he was trying to teach us something. Jacob continued asking what Cole was afraid of. I worried a fight might break out, as neither received an answer to their respective questions, but Cole and Jacob retreated to their corners. Jacob returned to talking about Dylan Thomas. Cole mumbled something about not liking to talk, which was true enough, and fell asleep.

I cannot say what insights our guest author garnered that

night about the lifestyle or character of young—and fairly privileged—travellers, but I suspect we filled few pages. Character is the result of self-reflection, itself the product of time and circumstance. He wanted something from us we didn't yet have; there wasn't even the wriggling sperm of an authentic self. There was, as they say, no there there.

I went to bed, escorted by the drumbeat of a marching headache. The next morning, our guest was gone. I never met him again. But two years later, while rummaging through a remainder basket at a Zeller's store, I came across one of his books. I still have it.

A few days later, we gave up the penthouse. I relocated to a campground, Playa de Toro, near Mas Polomas, where backpackers were quartered in wooden stalls along a dividing bamboo fence. The bamboo proved a useful material for making chillum pipes; my years in industrial shop class were not, as it turned out, entirely wasted.

A gate was opened early each morning and locked again late in the evening so as to bar unpaying guests from using the campground. High above the campground loomed a mountain consisting of sand, rock, low bushes, and more sand. The camp's guests were an eclectic bunch, mainly Canadians and Americans, a few Germans and French, but I remember only one: a guitar-playing ex-Marine frogman who told us he had a brown belt in judo and used to go on commando raids to capture people in Vietnam. What he didn't tell us, but was easily guessed, was that he suffered from PTSD. His hair-trigger temper could be awakened by an innocent comment or passing glance. At such moments, his Marine Corps body would tense and take on the stance of someone fighting his way out of a faraway rice paddy, clutching an M-16. Then, as quickly, the moment of rage would pass, and he would go back to scribbling notes, a wild-eyed time bomb waiting for the next trigger. He was one of a lot of wounded Vietnam vets nesting in the peaceful hippie getaways of Europe and Asia at the time. Jacob would have found him interesting.

INCIDENT IN A SMALL VILLAGE

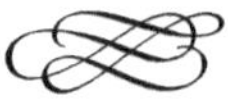

Still on the move, I hitchhiked a few days later from Playa de Toro to a small fishing village two hours by a semi-paved road from Las Palmas. I took up residence there for three weeks.

It was a sleepy village set between high mountains, a quiet place of fishermen and their families, the kind of abode Hemingway would have written about between wars, bullfights, and alcohol, the latter an activity vigorously engaged in by the village's locals and tourists. The lower village featured a klatch of small homes, stores, and cafes. The upper village, rising into the receding hills, was occupied by larger pensions and apartments, none of stellar workmanship. Unless engaged in actual work, as were the villagers during the day, there was little to do, an aimlessness that fit well the intentions of most of us non-locals. The exception was a small community of ex-pat artists, some of whom had lived there for several months, who spent days sketching while sitting on rooftops or on mountain hikes.

The community's main centre of creativity was an art museum near the waterfront. There, a passel of artists—some Spanish, local, and commercial, some foreign, itinerant, and avant-garde—worked each day in their own oeuvres. One local artist had a particular flare for painting pastel mountains shaped like reclining nude women ridden over by a skeletal Don Quixote and his paunchy companion, Sancho Panza, while leering faces leaped from the clouds or the women's tangled hair and windmills receded into the mist. Another artist specialized in surrealistic chickens; yet another, Turneresque versions of the swelling seas, mere feet from the actual thing; yet another, pastoral scenes—simple farmhouses, fields of ripe wheat, and discrete lovers accompanied by a watchful matron—reminiscent of Victorian England. None of the works were bad. But one day, I stopped to watch the painter of Quixote and women's rumps as, methodically, he attacked the canvas, working so quickly his brush became a rapier, parrying and slashing at the assembled paints. Within minutes, he had produced yet another Don Quixote. I realized with some regret that the windmills of commercialism had vanquished the artist, who was now a mechanical producer of commodities.

My accommodation for the first three nights in the village was in a small *pensión*, already occupied by others. They graciously offered me the kitchen in which to sleep. The kitchen was a tiny room with a gas stove and two chairs. It was filthy with dirt, grease, and leftover food. On my first night, I learned I was not alone, for as soon as the light was turned off, the dark gave birth to hundreds of cockroaches, not of the William Burroughs variety, but real cockroaches—*Blattella Germanica*, to be exact. An inch in width and between one and two inches in length, they scuttled out from the water and gas pipes, the stove's undercarriage, and cracks in the plaster walls, searching for anything edible. I felt their busy legs scurry over my sleeping bag and heard a distinct clicking sound as they ate and ran or launched themselves in a gliding motion off the walls, furniture, and stove. The first night, I flicked on the light and killed several with my shoe, but soon realized it was a Sisyphean task. Too exhausted to care and without any other place to sleep, I pulled my sleeping bag firmly over my head. Suffocation seemed a better fate than being supped over by a frenzied army of cockroaches. In the morning, they were gone again, back to their subterranean quarters.

On the fourth day, I moved to the *pensión*'s second floor to share one of many adjoining rooms. The lone non-American on the floor was George, a Czech refugee with deep, piercing, almost sinister eyes, who spoke little and ran a small leather shop in the village. The large group of Americans included two Brooklynites, Enzo and Marco, college graduates who were working in the local banana field to earn enough money to keep travelling.

Owen was a blond-haired and bearded Californian whose room was music central as he owned an extensive case of 45 rpm records—David Bowie, Yes, Jimi Hendrix, Buffalo Springfield, and Bob Dylan—that he constantly played, stopping only to roll another joint or attend to hot-knifing hash in another room. Owen spoke in a west-coast patois that sometimes gave way to an anxious, drug-induced, high-pitched laugh.

Among the *pensión*'s other residents were a couple of Jewish girls from non-Brooklyn New York and two others from the midwest, and Joe, another east-coaster. Joe was recovering from non-contagious hepatitis and spent nearly all his hours confined to a room. The other residents kindly brought him food and sometimes—when he was awake—played games of chess with him.

During the day, I visited the cafes and art museum or sat on the beach, reading books and writing notes. A week in, I took up running the steep, winding mile road that connected the town to the outside world. On another day, a young American girl and I went with local fishers to catch snapper and sea bream, taking our catch afterwards to a nearby sandy shore, where the fish were cooked over a fire, before returning later that evening to the village.

Evenings after supper were spent reading or getting to know the other members of the community. Attracted by Owen's music "studio," our *pensión* became the hub of ex-pat life. While some residents were heavily into drugs, most, including myself, only casually smoked marijuana and hashish, though some occasionally also dropped acid.

A going-away party for George was held one evening. A girl with long, blonde hair, wearing a flouncy bodice, drifted in and out of the second-floor rooms as though not feeling at home in any of them. Her name was Oksana. Like many others, she was from New York. She had lived in the village for several months, spending her time writing poetry and painting pictures. But mainly, she was lonely, her loneliness wrapped in a vulnerable sensuality. I was smitten but said little.

The art museum aside, the village was not yet a full-fledged tourist trap, though it did increasingly cater to tourists, resulting in barely hidden, sometimes open, conflict. The conflict was entirely understandable. The village was small and traditional; everyone, even the children, worked; everyone also knew their place, their role. By contrast, those of us who were visitors-cum-tourists, though not obviously wealthy, were carefree and spent our time pursuing pleasure in the form of drinking, drugs, and sexual debauchery. Constant tension hung over the village.

When I arrived, the foreign enclave was still buzzing about an incident that had occurred on the beach days earlier. A male villager with a reputation for being unstable—it was said that he walked around with a bleeding nose on most days—had tried to persuade an American girl to join him behind some rocks and, when she refused, had attacked Owen, who happened to be nearby. Owen fled into the surf, pursued by the villager, who tried to crush his skull with a large rock. Eventually, five men from the village came and wrestled the deranged individual into a car and drove him away. The incident was dismissed as being the result of the full moon.

The full moon passed. The village once more fell into a deep sleep until—a few days later—it once again awoke.

The waking hour came in the early afternoon. I had just showered after my daily run. I was sitting on the *pensión's* doorstep, drinking a beer, when a long-haired German emerged from the nearby banana patch. He spoke excitedly about Angela, the mother of Manuel—more about him shortly—who was screaming and throwing things out of a nearby apartment that her family rented to tourists. She ordered all of the "banana-patchers"—slang for the hippie tourists who hung around the apartment—to leave. I tossed the whole thing off as a rather dull incident occasioned by heat and boredom.

But then, two of the apartment's American renters, Sandra and Eleanor, began talking to each other in breathless tones.

"Oksana has a lot of explaining to do," said Sandra. "Her and Manuel."

"What could she say?" asked Eleanor.

"And Janice encouraged it," replied Sandra, using the name of the apartment's third renter. "Inviting Manuel over for meals."

I was needing a scorecard to keep track of everyone.

"She (Janice) even took a letter to him once," added Eleanor, who wandered off to have a smoke.

I was sitting beside them, seen but not seen, the word shrapnel falling everywhere around me, but absent any clear picture. "I have come to this rather late," I said. "Can you fill me in?"

"A to Z?" replied Sandra. "Well, the thing is, Angela—Manuel's mother—came into our apartment and caught Oksana and Manuel in the bathroom. She must have known something was going on 'cause she just broke in—well, they do own the building—and searched the kitchen, and then went into the bathroom."

At that moment, Eleanor returned, along with Janice, who now defended herself against accusations of being an accomplice. "I didn't know. I mean, there are always a lot of people in the apartment; you can't keep track of all of them!"

"All I know," said Eleanor, "is that he came in to fix a chair, and the next moment he and Oksana had disappeared and then Angela came in. And did she beat him! She just pounded him, and he stood there and took it. She was screaming, 'Everybody out.'"

"He (Manuel) has a wife and three kids, too," said Janice.

Eleanor interjected, "I think both Oksana and Manuel have a lot of explaining to do."

By this time, aroused by the commotion, Joe had left his convalescent cave and was standing on the step above me. "What would they say? What's to explain? That he had fixed the chair and was now checking out Oksana's plumbing?"

The allusion escaped Eleanor, or at least she ignored it. "It makes us look like we were running a whorehouse. That's what everyone will think."

As if on cue, another newly arrived American, Chuck, arrived to say that, indeed, the story was all over town.

"How do you say 'tarred and feathered' in Spanish?" I asked.

Down below, the scene continued unfolding. Oksana, dressed in her usual Bohemian style—a descending white bodice hugging her ample breasts, a flowered dress, and sandals—was doing an end-run of Angela's apartment, trying to get back to her own place. But as she did so, Manuel's mother erupted like an enraged bull through the apartment door, screaming at the fleeing Oksana. Though my knowledge of Spanish was poor, the word *puta* rang out like porcelain plates figuratively breaking at Oksana's feet. At last, looking back cautiously, Oksana made her way back to her *pensión*.

It was a hot and muggy day, and I went to the *tienda* to get a drink. A squat, unshaven villager came up to me. He was very drunk. "Where are you from?" he asked. "Canada?"

"*Si*," I replied.

"*Mañana—finito!*" he said. His right hand crossed his throat like a character from a spaghetti western.

I ignored the threat. "*No entiendo*," I replied and walked away slowly in the direction of my apartment.

A while later, Marco arrived. He was, as usual, nonplussed by the events. He had already moved on. "There's a kind of party for the banana pickers going on at the field shack tonight. You wanna come?"

I nodded, "Sure."

That night, the workers sat around a long table eating fruit salad, eggplant, and fried octopus. The wine and beer and talk flowed plentifully and easily. Someone stated, erroneously, that it was Prince Juan Carlos's* birthday. No matter, he would have a birthday another time. Pacho, Ignatio, Francisco, and a couple of other local field workers were there, along with Marco, Enzo, and me. Everyone was having a good time when suddenly a group of very drunken villagers began kicking and pounding on the door, yelling obscenities, angry at not having been invited to the party. Their harshest insults were reserved for their fellow Spaniards. This continued for a while until, in an effort to appease them, someone opened the door so that they could see what was going on, but this served only to protect the quivering door. The unwelcome guests stood sullenly watching, even in their silence, casting a pall over what had been, until then, a joyous celebration of Juan Carlos's faux birthday. The intruders did not enter, but they did not go; like Banquo's ghost, they merely loomed.

Having seen enough, at last, Marco exploded in true Brooklynite fashion. "Okay, I'm getting pretty fuckin' mad. I'm gonna start bustin' some heads. Everybody out!" He began shoving the drunks, who teetered like tumbling logs out the door, shouting well-known Spanish curses as they left. Tension and silence gripped the guests.

Soon, the landlord who owned the shack arrived, demanding that Marco and the others leave. Marco, now calm, shook the man's hand and explained to him what had happened, how the troublemakers had spoiled a peaceful party, but we all thought it

---

* He was born January 5, 1938. What is correct is that, in 1973, he was still a prince and remained so until November 22, 1975, when, upon the death of Francisco Franco, he became king.

best to leave anyway. We left in small, separate groups, skirting the drunks who had come to our door. A larger horde of morose men had spilled out of Miranda's pub; others, no less drunk, sat like surly crows along a wall leading from the general store. The village men, young and old, conveyed a mood of quiet and wretched foreboding, at the heart of which lay a combination of moral indignation and frustrated lust. Many of us in the foreign community went to bed anxious.

The next day was cool and cloudy. The surliness of the evening before had given way to a carnival atmosphere fostered by rumours that Juan Carlos might visit the town. Spanish flags fluttered over the village, and work ceased except for those in the bar and some *tiendas*. Mothers strolled, and children ran, sometimes falling and scraping their knees and getting up to run again. Young men flexed their muscles for the young women to see. An old drunk wearing a straw hat talked animatedly to another old man, who hobbled over to a table. We foreigners sat on the same wall occupied hours earlier by angry villagers, passing between us bottles of cheap wine, the laughter and smiles growing with each swig. Enzo snapped actual photos of the people while Oksana pretended to snap photos with her open hands. Everyone laughed again. More wine and beer arrived. The day went on. A small plane flew overhead. "Juan Carlos," someone shouted, and the friends around him laughed. The hours passed. The prince didn't come, but the tensions of the day before receded.

~

*I*t was several days on. We sat on the rooftop of Oksana's *pensión*.

"I don't want to leave," she said, "but I'm lonely, and I know I can't stay."

"Lonely for New York?"

"No, just people, friends. I used to keep myself busy in New

York, doing things so I wouldn't have to go back to my apartment. But the loneliness has followed me here."

I knew what she meant. Travel is often a means of getting to somewhere or something that continues to recede every time you think you are close: an illusion, a desire, a wisp.

Just then, Manuel came by. He was doing some renovations in the apartment. He looked up; his hand gestured a tepid wave. "Oh, that's what I was looking for," she laughed, the laugh of cutting glass, a pained laugh because it was better than crying. "Between being a writer and a painter, I'm a whore," and choked out a bitter laugh again. I should have said something, but what?

Another full moon was upon us. Large and golden, it loomed, perfect, against the night sky, obscured only briefly by a bank of surly clouds. A few of us wandered down to the beach with our bottles of beer to listen to and watch the tinfoil surf break against the sand. Back in the village, the bar was still open. A klatch of drunks in the square became loud and angry as though prepping for a fight, but it never came.

The shuffling of transient visitors continued. A few days later, a farewell party was held for Owen. The loss of his cassettes was greatly mourned. The ex-pat community was moving on.

On my last morning in the village, I went early to Oksana's apartment. I was greeted by Hamish, a foppish artist from Toronto in his late forties. Aided by a government grant, he had rented a room next door.

"Is Oksana here?" I asked.

"It's pretty early," he replied curtly.

Suddenly, Oksana appeared in the doorway behind him, her body wrapped in a towel. She disappeared into the room and returned shortly wearing a white bathing suit. Hamish, his mood brightened by having an audience, began telling us of his latest creative project.

"I want to get the fishermen's reaction to that phallic rock," he said, pointing to a granite obelisk standing out along the shoreline. "I've taken pictures of it from several angles. I want to add something to it today, possibly a garland."

"Or daisies," said Oksana, a taunt of mischief in her voice.

"Yes, streamers. I'll put an egg on it!"

"Oh, yes, an egg. That would be great," she added, barely stifling a mad, delicious laugh.

"I'll break an egg on it later," said Hamish, his creative juices in full flight.

"Wonderful!"

Hamish headed off toward the beach. The sun was already stroking the sacred altar where soon a perfectly good egg would be sacrificed to Hamish's artistic vision.

"Egg on the rocks, eh," I said. "And he has a grant from my government. He's nuts—or a fraud—or both."

"He's also a nasty piece of work," said Oksana. "He sent his daughter away because we were too friendly. He told me he thought I had latent lesbian tendencies that his daughter was bringing out in me. He's a small man—and, yeah, a fraud."

We talked a while longer. I went back to my apartment and got my backpack, then headed to the bus station. As was the custom, a small entourage of well-wishers followed. At the station, they insisted on buying me rounds of beer.

Hamish arrived, looking despondent. "The ocean carried my egg away."

Enzo and Marco walked over. I felt a genuine sadness at that moment. Though we made promises to stay in touch, perhaps meet again in Greece, I knew that I was walking through a door that was closing.

A while later, Oksana also arrived.

"Write me here," she said.

"I will. I want to see you again."

"You will," she replied. And this time, I actually believed it. I shook everyone's hand, and when I came to Oksana, we kissed gently; her eyes closed.

Tipsy from the many beers, I squeezed through the bus's narrow door. My backpack caught on a hinge as I boarded, making for a somewhat clumsy departure. The bus engine throttled up. I tried to stifle my emotions. I forced a smile and waved to everyone as the bus began moving. Soon, their faces were out of sight.

BARCELONA, CON-MEN,
AND BULLS

*S*ome years ago, a colleague and I became spiritual brothers upon realizing, first, that both of us had wished we had fought—perhaps even died—in defence of the Republican side and against the fascists during the Spanish Civil War; and second, that we were both in love with Ingrid Bergman. My first fleshy acquaintance with the Spain of my dreams was in the spring of 1973, on my way to the Canary Islands. It was a brief romance, but rekindled weeks later on my return to the mainland when I hitchhiked from Cadiz along the Costa del Sol to Barcelona.

It was early March. Generalissimo Franco was still alive and would be for two more years. Coastal Spain was already, as Paul Theroux would later describe*, the victim of a powerful, modern colonization, a playground for foreign—but mainly British, and especially English—tourists: campsites and caravans, beach umbrellas, beer tents, and English pubs.†

---

* *The Pillars of Hercules* (New York: Fawcett, 1995).

† Simon Grayson's, *The Spanish Attraction: The British Presence in Spain from 1830 to 1965* (Malaga: Santana, 2001) details how British political, cultural, and economic influence has a long history in Spain. Especially in Andalusia, though also in Catalonia, British investment both stimulated and limited the country's

Yet, outside of the tourist haunts of Torremolinos and Malaga, much of southern Spain seemed unchanged from black-and-white postcards of the 1930s. A profound grimness hung over everything: colour—life—sucked and drained from streets and buildings, from flowers and trees, from people's faces. Older people seemed gripped with a pensive fear that, at any moment, the shelling must *surely* be about to resume. Children played hesitantly, and young girls of fifteen, on the doorstep of ripening womanhood, gave only momentary smiles. Angst, mixed with bland hopelessness, clung like suet over daily life; death masks watching, shades of the other Bergman.

But Barcelona was different. True, the city had taken the brunt of Franco's ferocity, aided and abetted by internecine conflicts among anarchists, communists, and socialists. The walls of some buildings still bore rhythmically patterned bullet holes. Green-khakied soldiers, wearing Wehrmacht hand-me-downs and helmets and looking bored, stood on guard or rode past in troop carriers. The Guardia Civil officiously strutted the city streets, checking people's papers and handing out parking tickets. They were joined by pairs of white helmeted American MPs carrying billy clubs, looking for wayward US sailors.

One afternoon, while strolling, I met some American servicemen from the USS aircraft carrier *Intrepid*, making its final tour of the Mediterranean before going home to be mothballed. They invited me aboard for a tour of the aircraft carrier, taking me down into its bowels to see the hydraulics of how planes were brought up from below for takeoff.*

Escaping the rest of Spain's greyness, however, there was colour; there was laughter; amidst rampant Catholicism, there was even the hint of sin. In the face of defeat, the Catalans had

---

economic development. Mass tourism, beginning in the 1960s, brought a new wave of British cultural influence.

* Xavier Theros's *La Sisena Flota a Barcelona* (Barcelona: La Campana, 2010) contains a history of the US Sixth Fleet's presence in Barcelona from the early 1950s until the end of the 1990s.

not succumbed. This was the Barcelona to which I arrived in early March 1973 and where I stayed the next month.

As luck would have it, I bumped into Owen from the Canaries almost as soon as I arrived. He had driven to the city in a van and was settled in a third-floor apartment above a consulate just off Las Ramblas. The apartment had an elevator, but most days, I took the stairs as the lift was cramped and slow and wheezed a death rattle in its struggle to reach each floor. Owen's room was a double, and so, despite his dangerous proclivity to drug use in a country harshly punitive in that regard, penury led me to lodge with him.

The room had no windows, yet without fail, I could sense what kind of day it was. On sunny days, dogs in the narrow street below barked, and car horns blared. Garrulous people shouted, and shop doors slammed with boisterous vitality. On cold, bleak days, I woke to a dismal silence that would chase me out of the apartment even quicker. Dressed in jeans and a t-shirt, I would descend the bleak steps to look out through the main door's iron grates at the empty streets and park benches, hearing the constant drizzle of rain from the consulate eaves and watching the splash of vagrant cars rolling through the puddles; then, hunched into my collar, hands in pockets, I would search to find an open nearby café.

Owen rarely left the room, content to smoke pot or, when I was there, to expound on eastern religion, the benefits of various drugs, and the wisdom of Timothy Leary. He had a ready cache of epigrams that he would bring out between nervous bouts of laughter.

"The smaller the man, the bigger the crutch."

"Tell me the truth, but if I can't take it, tell me a good lie."

An elderly couple managed the apartment. He was perpetually glum, never smiling; his utterances were mere mumbles to himself. She talked continuously and often asked me questions I did not understand, to which she would reply, "*Si, si,*" or, likewise, "*No entiendo,*" and then laugh. Still talking, she would sometimes burst randomly into our room to make our beds or replenish the drinking water, then carry on fussing about and talking to herself or making a whistling sound indistinguishable from a song or an asthmatic wheeze.

She and her husband argued non-stop. One day, the dispute seemed to revolve around who would answer the phone, so neither did. Another day, they argued about how much to charge me. She wanted seventy-five pesetas, but he won at sixty pesetas. I hurried out the door before a rematch ensued.

I spent my first days walking the wide Ramblas or strolling the Marquis del Douro, stopping at a kiosk sometimes to read an *International Herald Tribune*. Threatened by an angry blue-aproned attendant, I sometimes even bought a copy. One day, I strolled the grounds of Gaudi's Sagrada Familia in all its unfinished splendour, staring up at the tenuous scaffolding. But on many days, I simply took in the city's sights and sounds—its feel —before returning to the apartment for a siesta. In the Spanish way, I would much later have supper in a small restaurant on del Teatro where I could get macaroni for twelve pesetas, topped off with a San Miguel beer.

By day, Barcelona's streets were filled with children dodging cars and playing soccer, the corners home to blind men and old fakers selling raffle tickets. Bars competed with each other, spaced only by pastry shops. The smells of fresh cooking collided with early spring's cold, smoggy air.

Las Ramblas was famous even then for its mimes, artists who wear make-up and costumes and pretend to be statues. They rarely move, and then only for a moment before returning to their stone-like poses. I watched each day the statue of an old woman—I came to call her Madame X—who was dragged out to sit. She was draped in a long dress, a high Spanish veil covering her withered face. Her right hand held a webbed fan. Nearby, a bored-looking young man dressed in a green usher's suit sat reading a newspaper, guarding Her Majesty from the teaming crowds of onlookers. At his feet lay a donation box. The stoically arresting woman attracted each day large throngs of watchers and their money.

By night, fresh crowds of people, released from the daily drudgery, emerged to fill the streets with renewed colour. Beneath the twinkling streetlights of Las Ramblas and the fading glow of café windows, older women in floral dresses bloomed against a chiaroscuro backdrop of repressed men in dark suits while young lovers walked the boulevard hand in hand, emitting their own spark. Roaming packs of sailors in blue leggings and white trim trolled the bars for liquor and prostitutes. On the del Douro, the garish neon theatre lights competed with the carnival play outside of buskers, pinball machines, punching bags, and coin-operated arcade games. Narrow side streets warned and welcomed unwary tourists.

Spain under Franco was authoritarian, sometimes violently so, as when his regime—materially and ideologically supported by the United States during the Cold War—tortured and killed its perceived leftist opponents.[*] The harbour was a dismal place of long-haul freighters spewing diesel and the American Sixth Fleet, given docking rights as part of Franco's quid pro quo with the US

But Barcelona hinted at other worlds. Tourists might bring unwanted glimpses, as did television and radio. The government's failures at censorship were not for want of trying. Like all authoritarian regimes, whether political or religious, sex was the first salient to be conquered. Even as the rest of the Western world was undergoing a sexual revolution, in Spain, the pill—and, of course, abortion—were banned. Likewise prohibited were X-rated films and magazines, such as *Playboy*, though, as always, there was an underground market for illicit materials. At select kiosks, travellers could purchase the *International Herald*

---

[*] After the war, Spain harboured hundreds of Nazi war criminals and received American support during the Cold War for remaining staunchly anti-communist. Enemies of the Francoist state were often prone to fatal accidents.

Tribune, but it was always a few days late, and editions were sometimes censored. The situation changed rapidly after Franco's death; seemingly overnight, Spain underwent a modernist revolution. It did not solve all of the country's problems—no revolution ever does—but the people did become largely liberated from Catholicism and the attendant curses of patriarchy and caste. In the years after I was there, Spain moved steadily, if uneasily, into the twentieth and, finally, twenty-first centuries.

~

It was an otherwise unexceptional day. I went to the Post Restante. A few days earlier, I had sent a letter to Oksana inviting her to join me in Barcelona, but no reply letter awaited me. I was strolling Las Ramblas when I was approached by a tall—by Spanish standards—well-dressed man in his fifties, slightly greying.

"Excuse me, sir," he said politely. "Would you tell me how much money I have here?" He shoved a folded wad of American bills into my hand. I dutifully counted the denominations: three twenties, one ten, two one-dollar notes.

"Seventy-two dollars," I said and handed the bills back to him.

"How much is that in pesetas, please?"

I had recently been to an Exchange office and had a rough idea. "Seventy-two times about fifty-seven, whatever that comes out to."

"Well, you see," he continued, "I was given this by some American sailors to buy something, but I cannot change the money at a bank without a passport." He explained in response to my inquiry that Spanish law prevented its citizens from changing American money. "Can you change this money for me?"

"I haven't nearly enough money to do that," I replied. By now, my antennae were twitching. Sailors? Laws?

"Well, tell me how much you have."

"I haven't enough." His insistence made my antennae reverberate even greater.

"Well, give me what you have then."

"No, it wouldn't be fair to you," I said. By now, I was certain he was several shades of the species "crook."

"Please," he said.

"No," I retorted sharply and walked away. I walked back to the apartment, where Owen reclined, half-stoned, on his bed. I told him the story. "There was just something wrong about it."

"Well, I would've taken him up on it," he said in his California twang. "I'd have risked at least a thousand pesetas. You might have made sixty dollars profit!"

We talked no more of it. Owen relaxed into his daily routine of smoking marijuana and declaiming on the meaning of life. I spent the next few days reading my books and the odd *International Herald Tribune* I had finally conceded to buy. Two stories dominated its pages: the winding down of the American presence in Vietnam and the winding up of the Watergate scandal.

It was early afternoon three days later. I went for breakfast but was tired and returned early to the apartment for a siesta. Because Owen was off that day to sell his van, I expected to have the room to myself. Instead, when I walked in, Owen was sitting on the bed. He was more agitated than usual and was veering from hysterical laughter to angry tears and back again.

"I've been took," he said. Crumpled on the bed beside him were several folded pieces of paper. "That fucking Spaniard must have changed them in his pocket! I just paid forty-two hundred pesetas for this fucking paper."

"I told you he was a crook," I said unsympathetically.

"But I counted it: ninety-two dollars. That son of a bitch."

I stifled an urge to laugh. "How did you pay him?"

"With the money from the van."

"How much did you sell it for?"

"A hundred."

"And you gave him eighty?"

He nodded, on the verge of tears and hysterics again. "I got this one American dollar that covered the folded paper, that's all." He looked at the scornful eagle. "That goddamn son of a bitch."

~

My time in Barcelona was ending. There was still no word from Oksana. I had to accept that she was not going to join me. Owen had left days earlier, so the room in the apartment was also eating into my money. It was time to move on. I bought a train ticket heading north.

It was a cool morning: Sunday, the first of April. The world was still buzzing with word that the previous night, Muhammad Ali, his jaw broken, had suffered defeat at the hands of Ken Norton. Ali was my hero. It was not a good start to the day.

I walked in the Parque de Montjuic. Early afternoon came. The sky was clear and cool. Standing on the corner of the Placa d'Espanya, I saw the bullfighting arena, Las Arenas, built in 1900, the first in Barcelona. Bullfighting was always held on Sundays when in season. Buildings, lamp posts, and restaurant walls were plastered with colourful posters featuring balletic matadors, advertising the *corrida de toros* of that day.

Catalonia banned bullfighting in 2011, but it was still popular throughout Spain in 1973. The Franco government was still putting money and political support behind it. Bullfighting was viewed as reflecting an essential element of Spanish character and identity. Until that Sunday, I had resisted the idea of taking in a bullfight but decided now that I would. I bought a cheap ticket from a grim gentleman behind the arena's sales window, who stared at me through a wire mesh: thirty pesetas, about fifty cents.

Why did I do it? It was more than morbid curiosity, something else. I had not then heard the Roman playwright Terence's remark, "I am human; I consider nothing human alien to me," but it captures something of my motivation. I was in Spain, and bullfighting meant something to Spanish people*, to their culture, so I convinced myself that I should set aside my prejudged abhorrence and take in the spectacle simply because it was a spectacle.

The man behind the wire mesh said the bullfights would begin at 5 p.m., but at a different arena, la Plaza de Toros Monumental, close to the Sagrada Familia. I walked away, now uncertain whether I would go. I fumbled the crumpled ticket in my pocket. *A wasted thirty pesetas*, I thought. I sought out a nearby restaurant and ordered a *café con leche* from a tall, gaunt waiter whose thick lips and sleepy bearing seemed chosen for the cold day. I read a book to kill time, at last, paid my bill, then made my way to a metro stop to take me to my appointment with tradition and custom.

Somewhere along the way, I heard Hemingway speak. "It's a good and true day," he said. I did not disagree. We boarded the subway train together, got off a few blocks later, and walked the remaining abbreviated distance to the stadium. Then, suddenly, as quickly as he had appeared, Hemingway vanished.

From outside, the stadium looked like every sports stadium everywhere since the Romans made the Colosseum: a high outward-facing stone wall topped with arched doors and porticos. Before the main gates, a sea of people gathered, eating and drinking, amid the sounds of blaring horns, cheering, and eager sellers hassling customers. Sombre Guardia Civil policed the entrances and exits. I was greeted inside by friendly blue-capped ushers and blank-faced ticket collectors. It could have been a North American baseball game.

---

* Carlos Fuentes, one of the twentieth century's greatest Spanish-American writers, argues the bullfight is an "erotic event," in which the bullfighter strikes provocative sexual poses, flaunting his sexual organ, in a "lust for blood and sensation." Carlos Fuentes, *The Buried Mirror: Reflections on Spain and the New World* (New York: First Mariner Books, 1999).

Locating my port of entry, I scaled four flights of stairs. I passed a first tier of plastic blue seats, perhaps a third of the stadium's nearly 19,000 seats; then on to the arena's second tier, where I was greeted by a short, overweight usher who showed me to my cheap seat or, rather, a number painted on a cement bleacher.

From my seat, I saw, just over the wall, two spires of the Sagrada Familia. Below me, the bullring was surrounded by a barn-red wooden wall, roughly seven feet in height and marked at four points by escape walls, behind which the toreadors could hide from attack. The walls were awash with advertisements: Coca-Cola, Skol, Danone, and several movies. The arena floor was comprised of sand (not deep) and circumscribed by two white rings or circles, giving the appearance of a target.

I was there early, and so I faced the jostling of arriving spectators fighting over their place on the cement. Concessionaires appeared, selling peanuts, popcorn, and drinks. One enterprising man sold camera film. I bought some ruddy-red shelled sweet peanuts and waited.

An American couple from Wisconsin sat beside me. It was their third bullfight. As a water truck came out to dampen and pack the field, I asked them what to expect.

"It's pretty gruesome," the man said. "First, the banderilleros stick darts into the area above the bull's shoulders. This weakens him so that he can't easily rear his head. Then, the picadors ride out on horses and stab the bull with their lances. By the time the matador steps into the ring, there isn't much left of the bull, to be honest. It's pretty sad, really. The bull comes out all full of fight, and fifteen minutes later, he's dead."

The American's play-by-play proved accurate.

A typical program involves six bullfights, with each of three matadors engaged in two events. This day, as on others, two banderilleros, three picadors (riding broad-chested horses), and the matadors on foot strutted onto the arena floor. They took their bows before the cheering crowd and doffed their hats; they were the "team," or *cuadrilla*. They were joined by what the American termed the matador's "assistants" and a *mozo de espada*, or "lad of the swords," whose role was to supply the matador with his choice of weapon. The initial ceremony complete, all disappeared again into the stadium's subterranean quarters.

All at once, a black bull, a ribbon set on its shoulders, roared out from a pen and onto the arena floor. For a moment, it halted, surveying the flickering gold and magenta cape of an assistant lurking behind a barricade, then lunged and charged where the man hid. This lasted a minute before the two banderilleros entered.

One confidant and sure-footed banderillero carried a single two-foot-long pike in each of his hands, each pike of alternating red and yellow colours. He quickly drew the bull's attention, springing in the air several times before landing on his toes. The annoyed bull attacked, but the agile banderillero easily stepped aside. The second banderillo joined in the dance, then made a final pirouette, elevating high in the air, before plunging his spikes into the bull's shoulders. A scarf of blood appeared above the bull's shoulders. The banderilleros, not yet satisfied with their work, stuck four more spikes into the embattled wound, though three would fall out before the fight was ended.

The gates opened and the picadors rode out to the sounds of a brass band playing and the crowd's fevered chorus of, "*Olé! Olé!*" Two of the picadors stood aside. The other, wearing a sombrero and holding his lance, or *vara*, under his right arm, rode out on a large white stallion. The horse was draped in a heavy, leather protective covering, or *peto*, and soon drew the bull's attention. The bull charged, butting its horns into the horse's underbelly, while the rider stabbed fitfully above the bull's shoulders to sever and weaken its muscles. The thin red scarf became, at last, a gushing stream, but the crowd was unimpressed. The picadors had evidently done a poor job. Amidst hoots of derision, they departed, leaving the snorting bull to take centre stage, flinging its head hopelessly at the vanishing ghosts of the assistants' capes.

It was now time for the matador to issue the *coup de grace*. In a surprise, however, he was one of the banderilleros; evidently, there was a labour shortage, as this was the case throughout the remaining matches as well. In any case, the matador cast his hat onto the arena floor; the final stage began. At first, he played with the bull, letting it charge fruitlessly at the mocking cloth while he stood scant metres away. Gradually, however, the bull became immobile from fatigue. The matador passed his cape over the bull's head several times and was able to bow before it and even touch the bull's horns, unafraid. With his chest thrust out, the matador bent toward the bull and, like a swaggering drunk, turned his back and strolled away, dragging the limp cloak behind him while waving to the cheering crowd. He then abruptly returned to the bull. Taking its measure, he walked over to a station at the arena's edge and took from a young boy a white sword, which he hid beneath his cape.

"The bull hasn't long now," said the American, who was now well into his role as colour commentator. The matador approached the beaten creature, still hesitant; the crowd, spellbound, suddenly quieted. The bull made a few last thundering charges; then, the matador held the sword high in a stiff overhand pose at the bull's neck. Silence, a cease of motion, time suspended, then the thrust. The sword sunk immediately deep to its hilt into the bull's neck.

But the bull did not immediately die, instead charging again, pikes flying off its back and waving like peacock feathers spreading in the wind. The matador's assistants raced out in their pink capes to distract the wounded animal and preserve the elegance of victory. A few final, dusty lunges, the tossing of its horns toward its tormenters, and then suddenly, the bull's legs buckled. The bull crumpled to the arena floor, fitfully trying one more time to rise again. A banderillero rushed forward and thrust the blade of a heavy dagger into the back of its head, and all movement ceased. One of the bull's ears was cut off, the spurt of blood wiped off on the carcass. Three great stallions were brought out to drag the corpse out of the arena.

By way of justification, the American commented that "the meat is given to the poor." Meanwhile, several white-dressed attendants rushed out to rake the sand. The second bout soon commenced.

The second bull was large and gained the crowd's praise late in the match when it nearly gored the matador, who was trapped along the boards. The latter took a prone position while his assistants scurried out, waving their capes to distract the bull until the matador escaped. In the end, the bull died quickly from a single thrust of the matador's white sword.

Hemingway wrote that the artistry of bullfighting depends upon a "good bullfighter and good bulls."* The third fight fell well short of Hemingway's requirements. The picadors and banderilleros had done their work too well. The bull's haunches were already crimson with ribbons of blood before the matador entered. Scarcely standing, weak from exhaustion, torrents of blood soaking its mane and the dirt around it, the bull ignored the matador and instead stumbled and pulled itself to the arena wall where—alone, lost, no doubt confused and in pain—it rested its head piteously on a cement curb. The matador, sensing his own humiliation, stood mere feet away, taunting and berating the sad beast, but to no avail. At last, the matador gave up pleading with the bull and drove home the white sword. The crowd rose. Faint cheers were mixed with boos, the focus of the crowd's displeasure unclear. The matador gave a fleeting smile, bowed and waved his hat, then took the customary stroll around the arena. A small scattering of red roses tumbled to the floor, indistinguishable from bull's blood.

It was now halftime. Like at a baseball or football game, concessionaires walked the aisles selling food and drink. Below, a

---

* Ernest Hemingway, *Death in the Afternoon*. Charles Scribner, 1932.

water truck dampened the arena's surface. The American continued in his broadcasting role.

"The horses get gored pretty bad sometimes," he said, "so their vocal cords are cut to blunt the screams. I understand the sounds are otherwise pretty loud and horrendous." I acknowledged sarcastically this thoughtful gesture aimed at the fragile sensibilities of spectators. The American went on. "The horse's ears are also stuffed with cloth or paper, so they can't hear the crowd or the sounds of the bull. And they're also masked, so they can't see what's happening." Another silence, ending with a brief aside. "The horses are actually pretty old and on their way to the glue factory anyway."

The events began anew. The fourth and fifth bullfights proceeded much as the earlier matches, except that the bull in fight number five, while charging low, stuck his horns into the arena floor, resulting in a remarkable somersault. He landed flat on his back, then rolled onto his side before shaking away his dizziness and rising to renew his fatal, hopeless task.

The sixth fight began with the same ritual procession. The bull was shiny, black, and vigorous and in the early moments, seemed to be enjoying its unfocused charging and thrashing. This changed, however, with the appearance of the banderilleros. The bull proved difficult; the pikes were poorly placed.

The bull charged with serious intent and struck the lead picador's horse, low in its soft underbelly. The bull pushed the mount back toward the arena wall while lifting it like an industrial tractor moving a large mound of earth. The gouged horse's contorted face reminded me of Picasso's famous centrepiece in Guernica, its pain inaudible but no less obvious. The picador pulled on the horse's reins, perhaps confused himself that his lance, which struck well, had failed to slow the bull. Instead, the hunched bull struck again with renewed fury. This time, the horse's rear crumpled. It fell over backwards and then onto its side. The picador leaped up and scampered to safety, surrounded by the flying capes of his rescuers. The horse lay still. Was it dead? Perhaps it was only stunned. No matter, the still-incensed bull continued to vent its anger and celebrate its victory. It thumped again and again at the horse's underbelly until the banderilleros' capes and flags distracted it long enough for the stallion to be helped to its feet, apparently sound but not spry, and led out of the arena.

When the matador at last arrived, the shiny-skinned bull was still fiery, its nostrils still flaring. Viewing his new tormenter, the bull briskly charged the matador's cape. The latter, misjudging the still substantial speed and agility of his opponent, was caught flat-footed. In his haste to retreat, the matador tripped. The crowd gasped. The bull drove at the fallen man, who stapled himself flat to the ground. But the bull was less adept at stabbing than were his enemies and failed in two attempts before his tormenters in dirty tablecloths and bedsheets began flapping in his face again.

The battle began anew. This time, the bull, ignoring the magician's trick of an empty cloak, succeeded in gouging a banderillero. But that was only a brief victory. The bull wanted to live; it was a primal desire programmed into him. He would not go easily into the dark night. This the matador must also have sensed as he took his sword and buried it into the bull's shoulders, which now surged gory red. The bull's knees bent, and his body fell into a heap. He rolled to one side. One hoof pawed the air hopelessly as though seeking solid ground. His head raised slightly and perhaps his eyes took one final look at the world and the skinny banderillero running up to him with the icepick knife that was soon buried in the bull's spine. With an audible thump, the bull lay dead.

The crowd roared its thunderous approval, then hurried to the exits.

"We like to take consolation in the fact the bull is marked for death anyway," said the American as we left.

"We all are," I replied. It was just after 7 p.m. on April 8,

1973. There was a freezing chill in the air as I left the stadium. I learned later that Picasso had died that same day.

～

*I*n June 2022, I returned to Barcelona for the first time since 1973, accompanied this time by my wife, Terri. It was her first time in the city but, in a way, also my first time as so much had changed in the nearly fifty years. Foreign newspapers and magazines were easily found, though also now increasingly replaced by Internet and television. Women freely wore halter tops and short skirts. There were few priests or nuns to be seen. On La Rambla, a building called The Erotic Museum, adjoined by a sex shop, attracted passing attention from a populace now saturated with pornography. As in 1973, musicians, mimes, and costumed buskers still lined the street at intervals but played now to much larger crowds. Huge cruise ships, private yachts, and smaller motor and masted boats lined the vastly expanded harbour. The ships of the American Sixth Fleet no longer habited in the city, having moved on to Naples.

We stayed six days in the city. We did more "tourist" things than I had in 1973: going to the Picasso Museum, taking in a performance of flamenco dancing, and touring the Sagrada Familia, which before I had only seen at a distance. But mostly we were simply there, in Barcelona. One of travel's great pleasures is being; to enjoy a simple meal, to watch people, to meet with friends over wine—as we did. Or to have a brief conversation, as we also did one afternoon with our waiter, a young Pakistani man—angular, dark-haired, with a pencil-thin mustache—who, upon learning we were from Canada, informed us that, though he was not political, his two favourite leaders in the world were Canada's "president," Justin Trudeau, and his country's Prime Minister Imran Khan.

But often, we just walked, talked, and watched, sometimes taking photos, making memories. On most days, we did the tourists' march along Las Ramblas, from the Placa de Catalunya to the monument of Christopher Columbus near the harbour. They were two of the only physical markers that held prominence in my memory from years earlier.

But there was another one: the bullfight arena.

A quick search on Google provided information and photos about two former arenas. We set off on foot late one morning to see one at the end of Avinguda de Parallel.* We were in no hurry. The arena was not leaving, and whatever we saw on the way would be of interest.

The day was already hot and densely humid. Small shops, cafes, and apartments watched us pass. Suddenly, we saw far ahead on our left a massive concrete structure that, as we grew close, opened up into a fairground and convention centre. On the day we were there, Pride Week was about to start. Stagehands were setting up equipment. Rainbow colours and smiling people were in abundance—another sign that this was not Franco's Spain.

We strolled the grounds and then began our search again for the arena. It didn't take long. Ahead of us was a traffic circle, the Placa d'Espanya, and behind it, on the other side, the arena, now dwarfed by the onslaught of new construction. A dome now crowned it, but its red brick walls were unmistakable.

I did not fully anticipate what I would see inside. I knew the arena no longer held bullfights. I knew also that it had been converted into a shopping centre. But surely, there was something left of its past?

The answer was "no." The arena's entire innards had been removed, replaced by several levels of brightly lit stores and eateries connected by escalators and stairways. Coffee & Company, Swarovski, Swatch, Subway, Pandora, Lush, Mango: these and more occupied the space once held by raging bulls,

---

* Parallel receives its name because it runs (unlike any other street in Barcelona) parallel to the Equator (at 41°22′30″ North).

matadors, picadors, and cheering crowds. In their place, shoppers strolled, cruising for deals, or scanned their cellphones for messages over cups of coffee. I was struck at that moment by the deep irony of a former bullfighting arena now providing the façade for a shopping mall, itself the cover for bloodless consumerism.

Days later, however, back home in Canada, while reading my earlier notes, I realized my mistake: I had gone to the wrong arena! I had stupidly forgotten that, years earlier, I had been rerouted from las Arenas to la Monumental after buying my ticket. It was there that I had watched the bullfights in 1973. Today, la Monumental—renamed La Gran Corrida Cultural—still stands but is now a museum to bullfighting and a venue for large musical and sporting events. I was relieved. Few will regret the demise of bullfighting, certainly not I. But I also take some joy that an important part of Spain's history and culture has not vanished completely down a memory hole.

PARADISE LOST

2008. Our ferry eased into the harbour of Mykonos. It was almost exactly thirty-five years since my first and only landing on the island. I was now married with two children and settled in a university career. The ship bearing me and my wife was much larger than the one in 1973, but the harbour's geographic contours were the same if now captured by large catamarans, private yachts, and enormous cruise ships. The narrow, labyrinthine streets, designed in times past to frustrate invading pirates, now similarly frustrated tourists who, discharged for a couple of hours from their luxurious but predatory prison ships, wandered aimlessly amid a host of freshly painted (blue and white) shops and restaurants, gripped by the cold hand of merchants. And, while the island's famous windmills still stood, they did so now not as giants, reduced instead, broken, withered, and enfeebled, to picaresque symbols.

My first arrival in the port came at the tail end of my first journey to Europe, a journey begun in Paris, carrying through to Spain and the Canaries (earlier described) and then Italy, where —meeting by chance in northern Italy some fellow Canadians driving a van—I travelled south to Rome and finally the port of

Brindisi, from whence I took a ferry to Athens. By then, my money was running low. After a few days in Athens, I headed to the island of Mykonos. It was already famous, but not yet expensive for young travellers, and so offered the chance of extending my trip.

Greece's ferry service at the time was local and heavily subsidized to allow Greek citizens to keep in touch with relatives who had migrated to Athens. In consequence, the boats were far smaller than today. My ferry was a two-deck affair that travelled overnight and stopped at Andros and Tinos along the way. Some of the passengers were Westerners—backpackers—but most were Greek workers and their families, including children, returning with purchases, mainly food and clothing, bought on the mainland. That night, the small ship bounced like a cork, lurching and swaying, our fate in the hands of the Gods. Greek and non-Greek alike, we took refuge amid the main deck's seating. Children cried, mothers cursed, men smoked; in the dark, someone near me was heard vomiting. Untethered luggage spilled into the aisles like wayward balls in a bowling alley. I slept little that night.

Morning came, and the golden sun rose over Mykonos. Under its windmills' watchful eyes, a handful of backpackers, including myself, disembarked. Its port is tucked into the island's west coast. South and east of the town lie a series of beaches set like jewels amid rocky outcrops. A couple of my fellow travellers had heard of a beach, Paradise. At the time, the playas could be accessed only with difficulty. There was no reliable bus service, and the taxis that tackled the dirt roads did not run late into the evening. We caught a taxi part way and walked the rest over fields of granite boulders and limestone crags, past the low-slung stone walls built by herdsmen, behind which grazed donkeys and a dozing bull, till at last, the beach came into sight.

Paradise Beach is in a half-moon bay, encircled on all sides by a rugged span of unflinching rock. There was one small building at the time, a restaurant known simply as George's. It was operated by two Greek brothers, George and Freddy. Together, they had founded the campsite and restaurant in 1969. By 1973, Paradise Beach had become a well-known stopover for hippies travelling between India and Europe. George was a smiling, broad-chested man, dark-haired, with a moustache. Friendly and garrulous, he was the front man for the restaurant. When not conversing with the patrons, he would sit at the cash register, talking to everyone and forgetting the prices so that he made them up as he went along or simply give the food away for free. "For you, my friend," he would say. His brother, Freddy, was a thin and much quieter man. He ran the kitchen and only came out occasionally to bring meals to the tables and to see that things were in order.

There were others. Marco, a man in his early seventies who wore a fez, would run around collecting empty dishes from the tables. Sometimes, he would dance to rock music or waltz with the young tourist girls. He spoke no English but talked non-stop or sang Greek songs while shaking everyone's hand. And Dimitri, a small, frail man, perpetually nervous, who would say "Yes, yes" when the food was ready but shake his head, his cow eyes turning sad, when the food was delayed. And, finally, Marianne—I think that was her name—George's English wife, who, more than anyone, organized the place along a standard business model.

Behind the restaurant was a bamboo forest. While some people camped there, many of us pitched pup tents on the beach. Sans tent, I slept each night on the beach at the foot of a crest of rocks that sheltered me from blowing sand, huddled in my sleeping bag until wakened by the morning sun's heat and the scampering feet of geckos at play. On any given summer's day, perhaps a hundred young backpackers, male and female alike, made Paradise Beach their home. We were joined on occasion by day visitors—often a bit older and more monied—who arrived by small supply boats or two-masted schooners, come to gawk at the mysterious and naked hippies. Small aircraft with similar purposes sometimes flew low overhead. We returned all this interest with indifference.

My own tribe included a young woman from Toronto, a sometimes model, whose photo I later spotted in an Eaton's department store catalogue; two male cousins from Hamilton; a young couple from Ireland—rare escapees, at the time, from that desperately poor country—whose abode was a prehistoric rock formation above the beach; and a couple from Seattle, he a Vietnam War vet who recited for me e.e. cummings's anti-war poem "I sing of Olaf."

By day, we explored nearby coves or played frisbee football. The hot summer beach sand baked the soles of our feet, turning them into leather. Only the Mediterranean Sea offered respite from the heat. The water was cool and clear—as clear as polished glass—exposing an untamed aquarium of fish and coral, a visual feast for snorkellers. There were also jellyfish, one type of which had a nasty sting if touched. One day, a young traveller propelled himself backwards onto a rock and sat on one. He let out an anguished howl and launched himself off the rock, but not before the jellyfish had burned a circular tattoo on his buttocks that lasted several hours.

As the day wore on, all activity increasingly centred on George's. At mid-day, the heat unrelenting, we sat at tables under the restaurant's outdoor bamboo roof, reading, playing cards, and talking—just being. We ate French fries, Greek salad, moussaka, and dolmades. We drank beer, ouzo, or retsina, my first taste of the latter making me think of anti-freeze. The restaurant played music via cassette tapes—Joni Mitchell, Bob Dylan, CSNY, James Taylor, and the like. As day eased into the evening, the fragrance of marijuana and hashish wafted more strongly through the air. Occasionally, someone would bring out a guitar and sing. Campfires were lit. Gradually, we would drift away from the restaurant to our tents and bags to sleep, perchance to dream, and wake the next morning to repeat.

The beach generally contained us, though once a group of us ventured into town to dance and drink at the Windmill Bar, literally a windmill that had been converted into a bar and disco. On another occasion, word spread that the town's open-air movie theatre was going to host a film of the 1967 Monterey Music Festival, featuring, among others, Jimi Hendrix, The Who, Ravi Shankar, Janis Joplin, and Otis Redding. Such an event meant that pretty much everyone on the beach would be in town that night. Given this, George rented a bus to take everyone to see the film before returning to the beach and the restaurant.

A few days later, I left Paradise, catching a ferry to Athens and thence a flight back to Canada. In 1975, I met a young woman from Ottawa who had more recently travelled to the island.

"Did you go to Paradise Beach?" I asked.

"Of course," she replied, and we compared notes. "Did you know George died? He was in England with his wife—heart attack, I think."

~

The ship's great maw opened to disgorge hundreds of cars, vans, and lorries. On each side, a caravan of tourists streamed onto the dock. We were greeted by Christina, a charming blonde woman of German descent who took us to her pension high above St. Stephanos beach in Mykonos town.

Once settled in, Terri and I made our way to the bus stop on the town's outskirts. I approached a small kiosk, returning moments later, singing—not terribly original, I admit—that I had two tickets to Paradise. We boarded the bus, part of a great and colourful army of swimsuits, umbrellas, sunglasses, and day bags. The bus set off, stopping occasionally to pick up or discharge passengers. A half-hour later, we arrived at Paradise Beach.

We were greeted by a brace of expensive, white-washed rental pods, cafes, and tourist shops. A disco blared dance music. Hot and cold running attendants hawked towels, beachwear, and rental chairs. The beach's ambience was guarded, less free and spontaneous—more commercial—than in 1973. There was far less nudity.

I recognized nothing. Even the mountain that had once sheltered me by night seemed diminished. Paradise Beach was like a face that had experienced a terrible accident and undergone a failed reconstruction. But then, we came upon a small restaurant featuring a sign, *Paradise Beach Self Service Restaurant General Store. Est. 1969.*

We entered cautiously. My disappointment returned. "Nothing seems familiar," I said to my wife. The young man behind the counter dutifully pointed out what was on order: eggplant, French fries, rice, dolmades, keftedes. I said casually that I had stayed on Paradise Beach years before. The young man remained emotionless but then said something about Freddy and pointed to the cash register.

I turned. Though thirty years had passed, I recognized him. I carried my tray over to where he sat on a high stool. I pulled out my wallet to pay for our food and mentioned that I had lived on the beach in the early 1970s. The words scarcely left my lips when his eyes lit up. "Ah, the hippies!" he said and jumped from his seat to embrace me. Like George before him, he couldn't quite remember how much the food items cost, instead magically pulling a price from the air. We remembered George and talked about Marianne—she now lived in England but still came to Mykonos each year—and of the reunions of people from that time that still happened, though now less frequently and with fewer attendees.

Terri took a photo of me and Freddy and a couple of his staff.

We then took a seat at a table to eat our meal, delicious as always.

By Greek standards, Freddy was well off. The business he and George had started more than fifty years ago had been a success; nostalgia was a poor replacement. But for a fleeting moment, as we talked, I wondered if perhaps Freddy, like all of us, might have longed for a simpler and more innocent time; if perhaps the road much taken had, in the end, led to Paradise lost.

NEAR DEATH BY RABBIT

Hitchhiking was common in North America in the 1960s and 1970s. Scores of people would queue up for half a mile or more on the outskirts of cities and small towns on major roads and secondary highways. The phenomenon extended to much of the Canadian Prairies. Hitchhiking was a cheap way to get around, to meet people, and to collect stories. Hitchhiking had its own etiquette. One did not jump the line to get ahead of other hitchhikers—though perhaps this was a peculiarly Canadian trait. Hitchhiking is also an acquired skill. In time, one learns such things as what form of signage to employ, where to stand so that cars and trucks can stop, and how to make eye contact and read the drivers.

It was late afternoon, late spring 1974, eastern Saskatchewan, the Yellowhead Highway. I was supposed to be on my way home, heading west to Edmonton. But I was a forlorn creature, shivering alone on a rain-soaked roadside. My repertoire of songs, sung to pass the time, had shrunk through overuse. My army surplus jacket and denim jeans were drenched. Slapping my arms back and forth for warmth, I looked like a frozen soldier at Stalingrad. The sky was black and angry like a vengeful crow, its claws scratching jagged lightning bolts against the pitch darkness. I could scarcely see fifteen feet in front of me. Desperate, I stuck my thumb out at every passing vehicle but wondered who could even see me.

Until a small red car pulled up. The door opened. I couldn't see inside the car but got in anyway.

Slowly, my eyes adjusted. The driver was a lean man in his late twenties with long dark hair and a drooping Captain Beefheart moustache with sideburns to match.

"Where ya' goin'?" he asked in a Louisiana drawl.

"Edmonton."

"I can get you to Saskatoon."

"Okay."

My rescue vehicle was a Volkswagen Rabbit, with a standard transmission, of course, which my benefactor was determined to put through its paces. The g-force quickened. I looked over at the speedometer. The numbers ticked off in rapid succession: 60, 70, 80, 90, 100. *Geezus, we're going 100 miles an hour!* We were no longer tethered to the earth. The Rabbit was hopping over great rivers of thrashing water that bounced with a thud off its undercarriage and sometimes covered the windshield as though we were going through a high-intensity car wash.

Years later, I punched "Volkswagen Rabbit, 1970s" into Google. The following observation of a former owner appeared*:

The Rabbit was unpredictable on bumpy turns. Its excellent handling would quickly turn into uncontrollable over- or understeer with the addition of a few bumps or a hydroplanable puddle. This, and the lack of warning between "limit of adhesion" and "no adhesion," may explain the loss of so many Rabbits to side-of-the-road ditches.

And so it was. The sardine-can chariot carrying me skipped, bounced, and lurched through the pitch-black evening. All the while, my driver kept talking in an excited drawl, but I heard nothing. At some point, he must have sensed my fear.

"Don't worry," he said, "I own a Ferrari back in New

---

* https://www.allpar.com/threads/volkswagen-rabbit-1970s-and-2006.236932/

Orleans." *Of course*, I thought. *Why should I worry? Aren't Ferraris and Rabbits nearly vehicular twins?* He dropkicked the gear again.

Gradually, I was overcome by a fatal calm. Death held no dominion over me. I attended to his story, or at least the one he told me, the one he presumably told everyone, including himself.

He said he was a student at Tulane University, but in summer earned money travelling to work camps. There, he played pool, fleecing unsuspecting proletarians of their hard-earned cash before skipping to another camp. His earnings were not to pay for school, however, but to feed his cocaine habit. (He accelerated the Rabbit.)

The Rabbit was rented from a dealer in southern Alberta. The rental agreement stipulated a limited mileage, beyond which there were extra charges, but he had run the odometer back several times while zigzagging across the Prairies.

The rain continued to pelt. Through the walls of water, I thought for a moment I saw the outline of Mt. Ararat, but perhaps it was only the jowls of Mt. Diefenbaker. We sped on. The wild-eyed lunatic beside me played high hat on the steering wheel to the thump of water drumbeating on the Rabbit's undercarriage.

Death leered again. There was no choice. I must abide.

Suddenly, a sheen of light appeared on the cloud's underbelly. It was Saskatoon's halo in the far distance. Then, just as suddenly, we were at its gates. "Is this okay?" he asked.

"Yes."

He dropped me at a truck stop. I bid him goodbye and went inside to use the washroom. A truck driver was getting a coffee.

"Where ya' going?" I asked.

"Edmonton," he replied.

"Can I get a ride?"

Sure. His cab had an overhead sleeper. On his offer, I crawled up into it. A few hours later, I was in Edmonton, still tired but alive.

THE NEW ORLEANS BLUES

My 1973 Oldsmobile Omega hatchback, 350 Rocket humming, AM radio blaring, sped along the Missouri highway, miles from New Orleans, where I had begun the day. A silky mist of snow hung against the late evening sky, revealing nothing beyond twelve feet. Suddenly, a Picasso-like apparition appeared off my car's starboard side, part solid, part vapour, a pleading face and a stiff thumb. Who the hell would be thumbing a ride at 10 p.m., in this weather, on this frozen tundra?

I thought once, twice, then pulled over. The ghostly figure, carrying a small backpack, ran knock-kneed toward my vehicle. He was thin and blond-haired; I judged him to be just a little younger than my twenty-two years. He got in the car without a word. He was shivering; the cold, I thought.

"Where you going?" I asked.

"Chicago."

"I can't get you all the way there, but I can drop you close."

He said nothing. His pale white hands were beating a nervous staccato rhythm on his knees as if typing out a front-page story.

"Cold?" I asked.

The invisible typing continued. Much later: "I was robbed."

"What?"

"A couple guys. They had guns."

Did he want me to take him to a police station?

"No," he said.

I was relieved, in a way. I hadn't a clue where we were and wouldn't have known where to find the police. So, I kept driving.

It was the strange coda to the trip's end.

~

By a stroke of good fortune, I was visiting Dauphin, Manitoba, in the spring of 1974 when I chanced upon an ad in the local newspaper seeking interviewers to work on a joint federal-Manitoba research project. The project, colloquially known as Mincome, was designed to look at the feasibility of a guaranteed annual income, an idea that continues to attract attention today. Dauphin was the project's main site. I met the project's hippie director, a dead ringer for Rasputin, who hired me on the spot.

I worked on the project for twenty months, surrounded by hard-drinking farmers, conservative townsfolk, and a passel of temporary outsiders that included, besides Rasputin, a balding lothario who floated each day on a sea of marijuana; a crypto-anarchist who one day accidentally blew off two of his fingers; a beautiful Jewish artist; and a mild-mannered Scottish devotee of Maharaj Ji. I was twenty-one, callow, and quite naive, but the group welcomed me nonetheless.

The job proved a seminal point in my life. We partied and worked hard. I took up long-distance running. One night, an older co-worker blessedly relieved me of my virginity. I bought a portable Underwood typewriter and began pounding out stories.*

---

* On the same day the typewriter arrived, I also adopted a stray calico cat,

Infused by too much Black Tower, beer, and weed, one evening in December 1975, six of us decided to drive to New Orleans's Mardi Gras. As the day approached, however, the others dropped out until I was the last one standing. In a fit of obstinacy, I decided to go alone.

Now, I was doing it.

~

The distance from Dauphin to New Orleans is nearly 3,000 kilometres (just less than 1,700 miles). Shrove Tuesday began early in 1975, on February 11. I left Dauphin a few days earlier, guided only by signage, a simple map, and my instinct. The Emerson border crossing; Fargo, North Dakota; Minneapolis, Minnesota; Des Moines, Iowa; Kansas City, Missouri; Fort Smith, Arkansas; and finally, Shreveport, "Red Stick" (Baton Rouge), and New Orleans, Louisiana.

I didn't actually travel through any of these cities until I got to New Orleans—merely passed them on the interstates—but they acted as markers, trophies that I acquired as I went along. I was channelling Neal Cassady at that time, enjoying the thrill of the hardtop vanishing under me. Driving was broken only by pit stops for gas, cigarettes, and coffee. The radio was pumping out rock 'n' roll, country, weather reports, and southern preachers.

During usual Manitoba winters, the divide between roads and ditches is erased by white wraiths of formless snow, the wind finely polishing surfaces into surly black ice. On this occasion, however, the prairie's winter gods were sleeping. I thought I was home-free as I crossed the American border.

It was not so. A sudden freak storm hit the Dakotas, snow-drifts erasing the line between highways, shoulders, and freeway

---

which I named Underwood. A while later, Underwood gave birth to three kittens, Olympia, Smith-Corona, and Back Spacer. I continued to write stories on my Underwood—the typewriter, not the cat—until the early 1980s.

overpasses. The signage and my instincts failed. I was lost for several bleak miles before a small break allowed me to recalibrate and get back on the main route.

Morning came at last. The storm eased as I entered Minnesota and vanished entirely by the time I reached Iowa. Wired, tired, and testy, my weary pedal foot grew heavy, trying to make up for lost time.

All at once, I heard a siren squeal and saw flashing lights in my rearview mirror. I thought—hoped—the cop car was hurrying to catch some hardened criminal.

No such luck. I pulled over, and a grey-uniformed officer got out of his vehicle and approached. He shone his flashlight into my car and asked for my driver's licence and registration.

"You know you were speeding," he said, his words inhabiting a space between a question and a statement of fact.

By Canadian standards at the time, I was not speeding, but I was not in Canada. A year earlier, the United States had passed the National Maximum Speed Law, setting the limit on all interstate highways at fifty-five miles per hour (eighty-nine kilometres per hour). For a moment, I thought I might escape the fine based either on my citizenship or, if ticketed, by being allowed to pay it later after my return to Canada—should I choose to pay it. Neither avenue of escape proved open for me.

"You gonna pay it now," the officer stated grimly.

Another out. "I don't have any cash, only travellers' cheques."

"That's okay. We're gonna drive down to the police station just ahead, and you can cash them." He added, "And if you try to get away, I'm gonna put a bullet through the back of your head." He spoke in a flat mid-western drawl as though reading from the department's Standard Operating Manual. I believed him.

I drove the few miles slowly and cautiously to a roadside police station, glancing back nervously through my rearview mirror at the police car following. At the station, I tore out a couple of cheques, paid the fine, and then got back on my way.

~

As evening fell, I entered New Orleans's outskirts. Fatigue was locking down my eyelids, but fear gave me an adrenalin boost. Even at fifty-five mph, the freeway's pinballing cars were more than I wanted to handle. The six lanes were four lanes above my experience.

By luck, however, I found my way to a side street near Tulane University, mere miles from the French Quarter. I crawled into my sleeping bag in the hatchback's rear, waking only with the sun's morning rays. For the moment, the streets were empty.

I was too exhausted, too broke, too alone, and too unhinged by the size and squalor of the city to really enjoy it. I slept in the back of my car for three nights. Worried that the police might ticket or tow the car if it seemed a vagrant vehicle, I got up each morning and drove it to a different nearby street, all the while also worrying that I might forget where I had parked it—a near miss, as it turned out, one night when I went to a steamy bar and drank too much. Only good fortune brought me home to port.

Most of the time, however, I just wandered around, tired and dazed. I strolled through the marble necropolis of the Saint Louis Cemetery. I saw the lights of Al Hurt's and Pete Fountain's clubs but didn't enter; too expensive. I visited a couple of record shops, where I bought Muddy Waters's and Robert Johnston's albums, which I still own. But none of it really mattered; I was in New Orleans.

Fuelled by endless coffees, three days later, I began my return drive.

And now I was in Minnesota, beside me a scared hitchhiker whose hands kept moving like a rivet gun, his eyes wide open, saying nothing.

The miles passed. A sign came up pointing to Chicago. I pulled into a twenty-four-hour gas station.

"Is this a good place to drop you?" I asked.

"Yeah."

"Do you have any money?"

"No!" he choked. I hadn't thought of how he might hear my question, that I was shaking him down. "They took it all," he stammered.

"It's okay," I replied. "Here." I handed him twenty dollars.

He got out of the car. It was the last I saw of him.

Sixteen hours later, I pulled the Omega into my driveway in Dauphin, my memories rattled by sleep-deprived images of New Orleans, snow-swept blacktop, a threatening police officer, and a very scared hitchhiker.

MY MOVIE CAREER

I felt a sharp stab in my right calf, almost like heat. As suddenly, the pain became a dull cramp. I turned to look back at the cause. There it was: a fake—but still metal—spear, wielded by a fake—but remorseful—Hittite soldier.

"Fuck, sorry, man," said Jack, the New Zealander cum Hittite.

Being stabbed by a Hittite soldier is not a usual event. But it was just another day on the movie set.

*M*y movie career began by accident. Weeks before, my friend Dave and I had flown to Israel from Athens to work on a kibbutz in the Negev desert (see next story). Dave had been there the year before. The kibbutz was a secular one of the type founded by many European Jews after 1948. I am not Jewish, but it was a good chance to experience the country and recharge my energy and wallet before travelling on.

Work on the kibbutz was physically hard at times, but we were free to travel on weekends, and did so to the Sea of Galilee, the Golan Heights, and Tel Aviv. By far, Old Jerusalem was the highlight of these ventures, with its ancient walls, narrow streets, multiple faiths, and assorted shops selling clothing, carpets, and jewellery.

It was in Jerusalem one day that Dave and I were approached near the Jaffa Gate by a man asking if we wanted to be in a movie. His name was Robert Kawasmi, and he was—as his card informed us—a Jerusalem-based "extras agent." He approached us, I suspect, because we "fit" the film's needs for young, able-bodied male actors but also because we looked like we would work cheap. He was correct; we jumped at the chance for stardom. The work paid $10 per day, American, plus meals. The kibbutz was none too glad to let us take a break from rustling chickens.

Two years earlier, a group of entrepreneurs, headed by a British film producer, John Heyman, had formed the Genesis Project. The project's intent was to produce a series of short and simple high-quality videos covering the entire Bible, both Old and New Testaments. The videos and accompanying teaching and study guides were to be sold at a profit to synagogues and non-denominational Christian churches.

Within a couple of years, however, the project ran into financial difficulties, and Heyman partnered with Bill Bright of Campus Crusade for Christ. The result was a shorter film, termed *The Jesus Film*, produced for evangelical churches, that was released in 1979.*

The Genesis Project was only in its beginning stages in 1976. Dave and I joined a hodgepodge of extras from various Western countries. Each day, we met at a pre-determined location in the Old City to be taken by bus out to a location in the countryside

---

* It takes some searching, but the story of the Genesis Project can be found in *The New York Times*, January 26, 1979; and in Matthew Page's blog: https://bible films.blogspot.com/2010/11/genesis-project-luke-ch1-4.html

around Jericho. Most of the extras were male, but there were also a few young women.

The set was relatively stripped-down, certainly not what one imagines of big box-office productions. Strewn along a dusty dirt road were a couple of vans and cars, a lorry, and our bus. A make-up table stood at one end of the road, where we were given our costumes for the day. In my case, too, a smear of dark lotion was added to my Irish red skin to give me a more "Middle Eastern" look.

Initial enthusiasm among project investors was then at a high. Big stars were anticipated to be lured into it. There were unfulfilled hopes that Gregory Peck would be the narrative voice of God. Hopes that the project would be bathed in star power were not entirely unfounded, as we soon learned.

On our first day on the set, Chaim Topol*, the actor who played Tevye in *Fiddler on the Roof*, arrived for the shoot. He was to be Abraham. It came to pass that, as he came on set, we—the assembled tribe of foreign extras--broke into a loud and bois-terous version of "If I Were a Rich Man." It was likely not the first time he had been greeted thus. He seemed to pay scant notice.

Little was required of us extras. We had no speaking parts. We were not much more than suitably attired human props. The female extras that first day each wore a tunic and a shawl to cover their heads; the male extras wore only tunics.

At last, the shooting began. The seminal moment was when Abraham (Chaim) emerged from a large, striped tent and announced to his flock the birth of his son. The great multitude of male extras was gathered a hundred yards away as Abraham stepped out.

"Ben," he said with all the gravitas of a biblical icon, at which point all of us cheered loudly, threw our fists in the air, and cele-brated the birth of Abraham's male heir (even if through his

---

* He died in March 2023, age 87.

wife's attendant). As all of us knew that nothing we said was being recorded, several of us broke into loud, profane curses: "You fucker! You son-of-a-bitch!"the Hebrew for which is *ben zona*. Topol, if he heard, again paid no heed.

I learned an important lesson about the life of an extra that first day: your movie career will end quickly if you are filmed in a close-up but being part of the faceless multitude means you might get several days' work. The fact that Dave and I were very distant members of Abraham's tribe meant that we were welcomed back for work the next day.

On no day before we arrived did we know which part of the Bible was being filmed. Instead, each day, we were given our garments, provided with a rough outline of the day's story, and told where to stand. We did not know if what was being filmed would be kept or if our best celluloid moments would be left on the cutting-room floor.

On the second day, we were given loincloths and made to

stand in a pasture with various donkeys and sheep, who seemed comfortable in their roles. The donkeys, Dave, and I (top photo) memorialized the moment with photos.

On the third day, otherwise known as the day of the long spear, we were given our most elaborate instructions. Some of us were to be Hittite soldiers; others, Israelite shepherds. Six of us were chosen to be the former and given to wear iron-studded leather vests, leather kilts, and helmets. Some of us, including myself, carried daggers or swords. Others, including Jack-the-Kiwi, carried a spear.

The scene required us Hittite soldiers to run barefoot over a small hill and down into a small gulley, where we would set upon a group of unsuspecting Israelites washing their clothes and taking water, who would then run away. It was a scene of intense action, certainly more so than standing amid goats and sheep in an open field, and the director wanted to get it just right. The camera's focus was full upon us vengeful Hittites, who were then to make a deft turn to the left down into the gulley, to which the camera would then pan. At least twice, however, one of us made the mistake of looking into the camera before making the critical turn, so that the scene had to be done over. In fact, for various cinematic reasons, the scene was reshot several times.

It was an exceptionally hot, though typically dry, spring day. Every redo elicited a fresh stream of oily sweat. I thought of my worst days of football tackling practice. (Coach: "You call that a tackle? Do it again.")

It was during one of the penultimate remakes, as I turned into the gulley, that I felt the sharp stab in my right calf. I looked down at my leg. A small trickle of blood was oozing from a gash. The gash running laterally across my calf was not exceptionally deep, but it was wide, a little over two inches in width. Jack, still holding his spear, apologized. A flurry of other fake Hittites, make-up artists, camera crew members, and others closed in around me.

My calf muscle began cramping. A young woman from make-up suggested I should get a tetanus shot. (I never did.) Someone else asked whether anyone had antibiotic ointment. (No one did.) The director was getting impatient to finish the shoot. Finally, the gay hairstylist arrived, bearing a white cloth. I tied a tourniquet around the wound. I flexed my leg, got up. We reshot the scene. My football coach would have been proud.

Though my calf muscle felt a little stiff, I returned to the movie set on the fourth day. We were once again shooting an entirely different biblical story. The bus took us to a new locale, one with actual ancient paved streets and stately columns. I have no idea where it was, but it was meant to stand in for either Sodom or Gomorrah or both; it was unclear. My dress for the day was, literally, a dress. It was a costume of many colours and hugged my hips as though painted on. I and several other bearded males were told to dance gaily in the street, throwing flowers carelessly into the air, and generally being festive. It all seemed rather silly. Like the previous day, several retakes were required. It was not my best performance.

We were told at day's end that, while a few extras would be needed for the next day, I was not one of them. The rented bus took us back to Jerusalem. No agent pressed his card into my hand and told me to give a call. My movie career was over before it began.

~

About twenty-five years later, I noticed a small store in Edmonton that specialized in biblical supplies. Out of curiosity, I entered the store and inquired about the Genesis Project. Yes, said the clerk, he had VHS tapes of the series. Did I know which tape I might be interested in? I looked over the selection of tapes and, based on the provided description of contents, picked out one that dealt with Abraham and rented it for a few days.

I took the tape home and stuffed it into my VHS machine. I had no great hope that I would find either Dave or myself among the footage. The scenes were so brief that being cut out altogether seemed a far more likely outcome. But quickly scanning through the tape, I came upon the scene of a Hittite soldier charging over a small hill and into a gulley, a white tourniquet tied firmly around his right calf.

"ARAB WORK"

Dave and I looked down at what might, in other contexts, have been the large, abandoned basement of an unfinished house, but was instead the discarded corpse of a swimming pool. The hole was thirty feet by twenty feet and ten feet in depth, not large enough for anyone to swim laps, but, if restored, large enough to paddle in and to wash off the day's sweat. It required only the hard labour of removing several years' accretion of sand, mud, and rotting leaves and a watchful klatch of frogs who looked warily at us from their walled prison.

It was February. Dave and I had been in Israel for nearly two months, the beginning stage of travels that would take us, in his case, to Africa and in mine, to Asia. At the moment, we were living and working on a kibbutz in the Negev desert. On any given day, we tossed large haybales to the cattle, moved industrial water sprinklers from one soybean crop to another, or—under cover of darkness—scooped up by their feet the dozing residents of chicken coops for shipping. On off days, we travelled the small country to Tel Aviv, the Golan Heights, the Dead Sea, and Jerusalem, and (as earlier recounted) had spent a week in the movie business.

In the evenings, we read, listened to music, or just talked. We got to know some of the Israelis, though not well. Language was only a small barrier. In my case, I was not brought up Jewish, though the kibbutz itself was secular. But the fact is, we were not Israelis and never would be.

I had only a smattering of knowledge about Israel. As a youngster, I had learned of the Holocaust. My parents took me to see the movie *Exodus* at a theatre. And I had avidly followed the recent wars. But knowing facts doesn't mean actually knowing, and in the case of Israel, there are multiple facts, realities, and truths.

There was then a strong liberal-left and secular element to Israeli politics, as well as a centrist conservative group. There was also a small but vocal group of extremists on the right, many of them followers of the "Jewish supremacist" Meir Kahane*, as well as ultra-orthodox members of the Hassidic community.

Except in Jerusalem's Old Quarter and on urban streets or buses elsewhere, I did not meet any Palestinians. They were present, of course: workers, businessmen, intellectuals, and artists. I just had no occasion to really meet any Palestinians or, indeed, Israelis, except those on the kibbutz; again, the language thing. If I saw an Arab person otherwise, it was most often from the window of a public bus, passing young Bedouins who tended sheep while carrying large boom boxes on their shoulders. Most Palestinians appeared poor. Few walked with the confident swagger of their Israeli counterparts. They had the hallmarks of foreigners in their own land, which they were.

In 1976, the Six-Day War was nine years in the past; the Yom Kippur War three years in the rear-view mirror. Israel's two solitudes were growing more fixed.

Now, Dave and I were staring at the dormant once-was-a-swimming pool. Winter, even shorter in the Negev than elsewhere in Israel, was ending. Uncoddled now by rain, the *humseen*

---

* Achcar, Gilbert. 2023. "Israeli far right's plans for expulsion and expansion." *Le Monde diplomatique*, December, pp. 2-4.

winds blew in from the surrounding desert, swelling and rolling across the empty wadis, warning of the heat to come. Dave and I looked again at the neglected ditch that lay at our feet, a promise of respite.

With us was Benjamin (Ben), one of the few kibbutzniks we had gotten to know. He was a slight young man, maybe a hundred and twenty pounds, with a shock of black hair and an easy smile. His English was good, although, typical of many Israelis, his phrasing began at the back of his throat, producing an emphatic phrasing of consonants.

Ben was a dedicated learner and sat with us night after night, perfecting his English. This is a task of monumental difficulty for anyone from another culture, as what passes for rules in English are often unclear conventions—or suggestions—that come and go, seemingly at whim. "But why do you say it that way?" he would ask. "Because that's how it is," we would finally reply, realizing the unhelpful and absurd nature of our instruction.

Ben wanted to improve his English because, unlike many young Israelis at the time, he wanted to travel outside his small country. He had a joyful and friendly spirit. He loved Western culture, especially the music of the Carpenters and ABBA.

But Ben was more than just a pleasant young man. At twenty-three, he was a decorated war hero, having subdued a tank corps and presumably killed several Egyptian soldiers in the 1973 war. He was one of those rare people who had entered the mouth of Hell and seemingly come out without a physical or psychological scratch.

Now, Dave and I were looking down at the fermenting mix of mud, plant, and animal matter. We turned to Ben. "We'll clean out the pool," we said.

Ben looked at us quizzically. "Why do you want to do that?" he asked. "That's Arab work."

Dave and I looked at each other again. We had no need to speak. We were children of the Age of Aquarius. We didn't need an Enigma Machine to decode the meaning of what Ben had said.

That day, we nonetheless set about cleaning the pool. It was hard work. The unguent mud stuck to our hands, legs, and clothing, an oily and putrid sludge. Two days later, we hosed down the pool and filled it with water. But we never used the pool, nor to my knowledge did anyone else. In time, the mud, the sand, and the frogs would return.

The Negev summer was at hand. The scorching sun, unrelenting and unchallenged, stood alone in the clear sky. But, on the outskirts, the dark clouds were marshalling.

I left Israel weeks later. I have never returned.

A HORSE DIES IN KASHMIR

The horse's high, throttled cry pierced the cold Kashmiri night, floating over our tourist encampment, circling the dwindling campfire and puncturing the solitude of our canvas tents. "Why don't they just kill it?" said Joanne, sobbing. "It's so cruel."

There was no good answer. Time alone held the only response.

It was June 1983. I was travelling overseas for the first time in six years, the interim divided among university, an ill-fated love affair, and redeeming satisfaction as a youth worker in a northern Canadian city. As many times before, I had now left everything behind. I was part of a group setting off on a trek from Srinigar, in the region of Jammu and Kashmir, in northwestern India. Our guide was Rakesh, the owner of a small houseboat on Lake Dal, on which I had recently stayed. Veda, a pale, gaunt woman of thirty-five with a pronounced stutter, came along as cook. Besides me, there were three Westerners: Joanne, a New Zealander; Malcolm, an Australian; and Genevieve, Malcolm's French girlfriend.

We arrived on our first day in Pahalgam, a hill station on the banks of the glacier-fed Lidder River, on a trek that would eventually take us to the Kolohoi Glacier. A brace of bungalow-type hotels stood abreast of the raging white water. These hotels were occupied by Indian tourists. Of these, a Sikh shopkeeper informed me, thirty percent were Delhi businessmen come to relax, while the rest were newlyweds on their honeymoon. Western tourists, intent on trekking, stayed instead in one of perhaps seventy patched and dirty grey and brown tents situated on the flats between the small bridges crossing the Lidder and Sheshnag rivers.

Horses—small ponies, really—were everywhere. Their presence was announced by green, steaming piles of excrement along each footpath and bridge and pea-yellow rivulets of piss along the walkways. Pedestrians out for a walk quickly learned they came second to any approaching horse and rider. Corpulent members of the Indian business class rode the dwarf horses and casually abused them with relentless beatings about the crest and withers.

Our meal that first night, courtesy of Veda, was rice, vegetables, and chicken. The evening was topped off by Malcolm, who was something of an astronomer. Sitting under Kashmir's canopy, he traced with his finger the Great Bear, Polaris, Venus, Orion, Cassiopeia, and the Gemini twins, Castor and Pollux, to the white sounds of the river playing behind us. The moon's rays hovered faintly behind a mountain, as though forever—yet not completely—rising.

We ourselves rose the next morning to a thin veil of mountain mist. The sun's light was just breaking. The smell of woodsmoke greeted us. Veda had prepared for us a breakfast of omelette, chapatti, and coffee.

Soon after, the seven of us—we had acquired Mahmoud, a sparkle-eyed young man, as ponyboy—plus a horse began a twelve-kilometre walk to the town of Aru in the valley of the same name. Shards of clear glacial water cascaded from the mountain on our left and plunged into the accompanying river. Colourfully garbed peasant women and traditionally garbed men with thick beards greeted us as we walked. Herds of sheep and goats followed in their train, while wild-eyed buffalo—red-pupilled, with white irises like huge buttons—watched, followed again by more men and horses and donkeys and khaki-dressed soldiers bearing tents.

The road stretched upward. On either side were trees, felled and shaved, and stone-brick houses that clung to the hillside. The river to our left sank lower.

Our horse, loaded with tents, packs, and supplies, moved on with the occasional slap of a switch from the ponyboy. Veda carried another kit. Intermittently, we stopped to drink a water-lemon mixture and to smoke a beedi. The immediate roadside was a riot of small plants: watercress, puha (a type of thistle), and edible angelica. Further aside, the ground cover was of cow turds, green grass, small stones, and large boulders. Above us, pine trees, dark green cedars, firs, and junipers cast their shadow.

We arrived at Aru's outskirts around 11 a.m. A temple seat carved out of the rock by a Muslim sage many years before welcomed us. We ventured into the valley again, passed a water buffalo's whitened skull and horns, and then climbed upward into the pine-suffused woods, a thousand cones littering the forest floor. Around us, clover, buttercups, and the white petals of strawberry bushes competed for attention. It was in this lush and bountiful paradise that we pitched our tents.

～

We walked the next day high atop the pristine valley; below us, a fast-moving river bristled. Looking down, Malcolm and Genevieve saw beside the water, some fifty yards from where our tents were pitched, a chestnut-brown mare struggle to rise, then collapse again. It writhed and rolled on the damp ground in obvious pain. Descending, Malcolm and Genevieve went over to the horse. A mountain peasant, a man perhaps in his thirties, thin and unshaven, stood nearby. He wore a grey cloak, a skull cap, and white pants. His feet were bare. It was clear he was the horse's owner.

Malcolm asked him about the horse. The man shrugged. He spoke no English. But no response was necessary. The horse's condition was plain to see. Its stomach was bloated and severely scarred in a checkerboard fashion from the back of its legs to the area just beyond its midsection. These scars, looking like fresh burns, had festered, revealing open, black blotches of blood and pus. Parasitic worms wriggled in the open wounds.

The horse's every movement was clearly painful. It lay weakened and stapled to the ground, eyes bewildered and reeling, nostrils flaring. With annoyance, but also because he seemingly could not think of anything else to do, the owner used a stick to switch the horse, then stood back, nearly as numb as the horse.

Rakesh spoke to the man and told us what he had learned. The man had some time before burned the horse in an effort to cure it of some ailment, but the mare had only grown worse and today could not walk. He could not afford to pay a doctor to treat the horse and so was now relying on Allah's benevolence.

Joanne, Malcolm, Genevieve, and me paid the necessary forty rupees for the doctor and sent a boy to get him from a nearby tent. In the meantime, however, and despite Rakesh's entreaties to stop, the owner continued to flay the horse.

At length, the doctor arrived. He examined the horse, after which he provided us the following details. The horse's owner lived in a village sixty kilometres away. The horse was suffering from azoturia—also known as black-water disease—which attacks the liver and kidneys. Fifteen days earlier, the man had burned the horse in an attempt to reduce the abdomen's swelling. Seven days ago, the horse had begun showing signs of a parasitic infection, which now had spread to the horse's vagina. The doctor opined that the horse required massive doses of an antibiotic, without which the horse would soon die.

The doctor faced a dilemma. The horse's owner was refusing treatment because of the cost. If the doctor intervened without the owner's consent and the horse died—a likely result—he would certainly face demands to repay the owner. The doctor left, distraught if not entirely ashamed.

The owner, meanwhile, had introduced his own medical intervention: an incision in the horse's abdomen made with a stick or piece of wire. He then sat beside the wretched animal, beside the writhing river, occasionally stopping to again beat the horse. At length, Genevieve approached the man and, through our ponyboy, asked if he would allow us to pay to have the animal killed. The owner seemed to consider this and, a while later, came over to our tents and spoke to Rakesh.

"Yes," said Rakesh. The owner agreed to let us pay to have the horse killed, but we must also buy him a new horse. At hearing this, Joanne leaped to her feet and angrily yelled, "You stupid bastard! It's going to die anyway!"

Though not comprehending her words, the owner could not have failed to understand the hostility conveyed by Joanne's body language. Rakesh wisely chased the owner away. Genevieve and Joanne took themselves in another direction to cool off.

$\sim$

Cruelty has its own rationality, its own internal logic. To its practitioner, an action may not seem cruel. It is outside of normal moral judgment. It occupies a place beyond our regular lives that we hope we will never have to visit.

This was where the horse owner dwelled. He was poor; the horse was likely the only one he owned. He was not sentimental about it. Either the horse performed some work function, or it did not. The man's initial calculus was simple. He could not afford to pay for the mare's medical treatment; its fate was in Allah's hands.

But, as things evolved, a second rational, if also cruel, calculus intervened. The horse's plight mattered to others—first, the doctor, and next, the Westerners. The horse would either live or die. As long as it was alive, there was a remote chance it might get better, so putting it out of its misery deprived the owner of its financial value. But also, as long as it lived, the horse's anguish was a kind of bargaining chip to use with those who suffered from its pain.

And so, the day went on. Within eyesight, the owner continued intermittently to flog the horse. This, too, seemed calculated, for he knew the act bothered us. Rakesh, noting our discomfort, went over to the man and threatened him if he continued to hit the horse. The man thereafter began stroking the horse's mane with his hand but always watching our camp.

Throughout the day, the horse's broken whinny whispered on the wind but grew ever fainter. We all felt wretched. At last, I convinced my three companions that we should walk into the nearby town for a drink.

We returned an hour later. Fording a nearby stream and walking toward us was the horse's owner. He said something low and unintelligible but not aggressive to Joanne as he passed and waved his hand in a single motion. I surmised the horse was dead, for he would not have left it otherwise.

My surmise proved correct. When we got to the camp, the horse lay sprawled on the riverbank, its legs stiff, its feet barely touching the cool stream. The mare's eyes were wide open, its mouth parted in a toothy, rictus grin. Flies were already gathering around its gashed stomach. One and all, we felt thankful for death's mercy.

It was then that I saw for the first time in a nearby clearing a young, chestnut-brown colt and heard its shrill bleat for its mother, lying lifeless in the afternoon's fading heat. The lingering sounds of mother and child haunted us through the long night that followed.

The next morning, the horse's owner returned. Overhead, griffin vultures circled. Crows had already picked clean the mare's eye-sockets. The owner and another man tied ropes to the carcass and dragged it away.

Three days later, we trekked sixteen kilometres over fragile snow bridges to the base of the Kolohoi Glacier. Along the path, small rhubarb-like flowers and mint leaves burst the ground. To either side, red-bearded old men stood, small children—young girls with silver earrings and endless necklaces and amulets—asked for baksheesh, and tall, darkly beautiful women walked in ankle-length, rainbow-coloured dresses, balancing food baskets on their heads: a riot of colour and life, backgrounded by the shadow of a dead horse.

TRAVELS IN LADAKH

The Indian territory of Ladakh, encompassing nearly 60,000 square kilometres, lies between the Himalayas and the Kunlun mountain range. It borders China to the north and Pakistan to the west. The word Ladakh means "land of high passes" and is technically described as a "high-altitude desert." Its historic capital, Leh, resides at 3,524 metres (11,562 feet).[*] Given its inhospitable climate and terrain, Ladakh's population, even today, is less than 300,000 people. Despite this, however, it is a much prized and fought-over piece of turf, with regular clashes along the Chinese border and, though less publicized, occasional small-bore incursions from Pakistani troops into the western Kargil region.

Quartering troops is no minor expense. Perhaps partially in consideration of this fact, the Indian government opened Ladakh to commercial tourism in 1974. Thereafter, a trickle of Western travellers and domestic tourists gradually discovered the region. In 1983, roughly 13,000 Westerners and 2,800 Indian tourists made the journey to Ladakh. I was among them.

---

[*] Wikipedia, "Leh." https://en.wikipedia.org/wiki/Leh. Downloaded August 2023.

My journey began in Srinagar on July 6, shortly after the hike in Kashmir. I left behind Rakesh and his houseboat and went to the bus terminal, where a heavily riveted and hulking beast, reminiscent of a First World War tank, silently waited. Urged on at last by its driver, the bus snorted to life. The driver's assistant then waved us excitedly to get aboard. The bus's metal seats were raw and almost entirely devoid of padding; its shocks, too, as we soon learned, offered no comfort. Low and cramped as it was, we took solace that the bus was an A-Class vehicle, thus sparing us the sardine closeness common to buses of even lower rank.

Just as we were about to set off, a ragged beggar boarded. He slowly made his rounds through the aisle, passing out printed cards describing his afflictions. I took one and paid him a rupee. He exited, and the bus jolted to a start. The smell of cheap diesel fuel exploded into the air like a mutant flower in bloom.

The trip began well. Though the temperature was warm, the sky was overcast. Torrents of rain had fallen over the past three days, turning the mountain roads to slop, but such conditions elicited only minor concern.

The bus stopped for tea and lunch at the small hamlet of Sonamarg, then headed for the Zoji La Pass. Carved out of the Himalayas, the pass stretches 6.5 kilometres at an elevation of 3,528 metres. It is closed during the winter months due to heavy snow. In 1983, the road's narrowness still restricted it to one-way traffic. As well, for military reasons, civilian traffic was confined to only a few select hours of the day.

At the army camp, before entering the pass, we learned the heavy rains had caused a landslide and that traffic was temporarily halted. So, we waited. I read a book, then got off the bus and ventured out into the bone-chilling drizzle.

Wool-like mists encircled the mountains towering above us. In the foreground, the tiny village of Baltal hugged the hillside, determinedly picturesque against the day's bleakness. I entered a squalid and small chai shop housed in a tent but was quickly driven away by the proprietor's equal disregard for his customers and his shop's cleanliness. I returned to the bus. We waited.

Evening was now beckoning, and the bus driver faced a dilemma. We either had to make the journey then—it was 1930 hours, the night rapidly descending like bat wings—or wait until noon the next day. Our driver, more foolhardy than wise, was bent on continuing. What followed for the next one-and-half hours was a truly frightening ride, offset by scenes of spectacular beauty that briefly caused us to ignore death's hovering. The high, jagged mountains swaddled us in subtle evening shades of grey and white, broken only by fluffy clouds and snow peaks that whispered of crystallized salt. Everything had an unreal quality. The mountains seemed mere cardboard cut-outs against a pale blue background. On several occasions, the road cut through a diamond-like glacier.

Only the week before, a bus had gone over a cliff between Jammu and Srinagar in a circumstance far less perilous than we faced, with all passengers lost.* Our road's narrowness was made worse by the monsoon rains that had reduced it to a thick and slippery sludge. Undeterred, our driver kept a steady speed lest the vehicle stall, but sometimes a combination of mud, too much gas, and an improper climbing gear made the bus swerve sideways as we snaked around corners. I subsequently read a local pamphlet† that helpfully informed readers concerning the pass that "Skidding of vehicles is a normal phenomenon and luck alone is the saviour."

Beneath us, to the right, a sheer drop into oblivion beckoned. At times, the bus slid within two feet of the crumbling edge. At

---

* Death, often sudden and horrible, was a constant, shadowy presence, as I noted at the time. Trains might stop because someone had jumped or stumbled in front. (Impoverished families often live beside trains in India.) Diseases, including rabies, meningitis, hepatitis, malaria, and tuberculosis were rampant, posing a threat to all and sundry. Malcolm, the Australian, told me he had seen four dead individuals since coming to India, one of them a man whose throat had been slashed by vigilantes for being an alleged "thuggee."

† "Ladakh: Land of Broken Moon," undated, p. 7.

other times, the road's thin ribbon was reduced even further by another vehicle coming the other way. On one such occasion, a Ladaki version of a Mexican stand-off ensued, involving much yelling before the respective drivers negotiated the terms of passage—who would back up and who would proceed. The dark of evening both hid and increased the actual danger.

At last, we broke out of Zoji La. The landscape turned dry and grey until darkness enveloped it altogether. At Dras, another military post—reputably the second-coldest place on Earth in winter—we stopped to fumble amidst the dimming light to show our passports to the bored guards. This requirement was repeated in the heavily militarized area.

We arrived at the town of Kargil, Ladakh's second-largest city after Leh, just before midnight. I got a bed at the "Popular Cha Cha Hotel and Restaurant." Five rupees rented me a dormitory cot. Holding a small candle, I pawed my way into a dark room, searching for my bed. A drowsing inmate scolded me for disturbing his sleep.

We were awakened at 0400 hours. We washed and ate a quick breakfast of tea and omelette. A half-hour later, we began the final leg of our 234-kilometre journey.

Much of that day's travel blurred. The bus's rigid and cramped quarters and a child's relentless kicking from behind my seat rendered sleep a futile pursuit. But the terrain also imposed a prohibition on sleep. Its soft, wispy, mysterious clouds, the hard, clear dance of sun upon snow-topped peaks, and the muted shadows cast between them: these sights compelled attention. Nature had set below us a rich and fertile plain, along which flowed a verdant ribbon, the ancient Indus River, bounded by three great mountain ranges. The diffusion of light revealed a subtle glint of purples, reds, browns, and yellows, which both competed with and complemented each other.

~

*W*e arrived in Leh around noon on July 7. I took a room on the first floor of the Rainbow Guest House. The room was twelve feet by twelve feet in size and featured a small cot, an equally small table, and a simple folding chair. A torn curtain covered half of a window that looked out on an unkempt garden. A shelf was built into one of the yellow-painted walls, beside which was a light fixture whose cord descended within reach of the bed. A kung-fu poster graced one wall.

My guest room was one of four on the bottom level. The floor above accommodated five other rooms, as well as two small showers and a toilet. Like many toilets in Asia then, as now, it was a rectangular hole cut in the floor, through which deposits were made. A posted card proudly stated the hotel's water supply ran twenty-four hours but failed to note that it was invariably cold until the afternoon sun warmed the outside water pipes to lukewarm. The hotel had a small garden, home to two well-fed ducks and one lone chicken who, perhaps aware of its precarity, scuttered about the underbrush ceaselessly in search of escape.

The guesthouse's downstairs hallway was narrow, its walls a pastiche of posters paying homage to period rock bands (Wishbone Ash), Bruce Lee, and Indian cricket stars. Once checked in, the hotel's Muslim owner ushered me into a room where I was graciously served jasmine tea, bread, and honey. I sat upon floor rugs, eating from a small table set before me, surrounded by benignly smiling attendants.

Sufficiently rested and nourished—so I thought—and eager to explore the city, I set off. Any fatigue disappeared as I wandered, wondered, and took in the serene faces of the city's people. I quickly headed toward the magnificent sandstone Leh Palace perched high on the hill, leaping over stretches of broken rocks and stubble. Then, suddenly, my head began to throb, and I grew fatigued and dizzy. My chest and back ached, and my heart seemed about to explode.

Unaware of what was happening, I stumbled back to my room, where I collapsed on the bed and listened to my heart's pounding. My sleep for the next few days was haunted by a series of frightening images of nuclear war and murder. These only gradually subsided.

I thought at first that I was experiencing severe fatigue. Later, however, I learned that my symptoms were those of altitude sickness, a condition that, in severe cases, can result in pulmonary edema, leading to swelling of the brain, lungs, and heart and possible death. My rapid ascent to Leh, at 3,500 metres, had not given my body enough time to acclimatize—for my red blood cells to carry more oxygen.

Rest and water returned me to normal. Forty-eight hours later, though far from recovered, I resumed exploring the city.

~

Centuries ago, Leh was the capital of the Himalayan Kingdom of Ladakh and a major stop along the fabled Silk Road. The kingdom's rulers lived in the Leh Palace. The palace was built in the late 1630s, around the same time as the similar but larger Potala Palace in Lhasa, Tibet. Following Ladakh's takeover by the Sikh Empire, however, it was abandoned in 1846.

One evening, I and some other tourists navigated one of many serpentine paths leading up the hill to the palace. We bought tickets—five rupees each—at a small kiosk, each ticket informing us that there was a "Lama in charge," and then entered.

The palace today still stands nine stories high, but the centuries have not been kind. Time and nature have chastened the palace's mud, wood, sand, and stone construction.*

---

* The Archaeological Survey of India is slowly restoring the palace.

In 1983, I noted the wooden suspension beams had begun to warp and splinter. For safety reasons, the palace's upper levels, which had once housed the royal suites, were blocked off; only the bottom floors, once reserved for the stables and storerooms, were generally accessible.* Still, several rooms sported frescoes and painted pillars and beams, suggestive of the palace's past magnificence. From a balcony, I looked out on the town below and the high, majestic mountains.

From the palace, we walked to the nearby Namgyal Tsemo Gompa. A Lama dutifully banged his gong and smiled indulgently at our inquiries, though unable to answer any of them. A skylight illuminated the temple's main room inside. A bamboo fence enclosed a man-sized Buddha and several other figures, including Kali. Pillars were gaily hung with papier-mâché festival masks. Shelving on two sides held small boxes containing ancient Tibetan prayers and scriptures.

The next day, I went by tourist bus to the outskirt towns of Sheh, Thiksey, Sakti (Thakthak), and Chinde to visit their temples and stupas.† The one at Thiksey was enormous and well-preserved. (A tourist booklet stated that it was "once ruled by a mad monk who thought of embracing Christianity but turned a highway robber later on." I wrote that the change seemed not a huge stretch.)

The Chinde temple was snuggled magnificently between mountains. It begged to be scaled, but as it was the end of a very long day, I declined the invitation. Instead, I took in a play—a parody of marriage—that was performed in a tented theatre

---

* The Russian artist and theosophist, Nicholas Roerich, his wife, Helena, and their son, George, along with a hired entourage, visited Leh in the mid-1920s as part of a Central Asian expedition. Author Jacqueline Decter (1997: 125) notes in her biography of Roerich, *Messenger of Beauty: The Life and Visionary Art of Nicholas Roerich* (Rochester, Vermont: Park Street Press, 1997), p. 125:

The expedition spent about two months in Ladakh. The vizier of the region invited the Roerichs to stay in his palace, offering them the top floor of the eight-story residence, which was built on a cliff overlooking Leh . . . The top floor often swayed in the wind, and while the Roerichs were in residence, one of the walls caved in.

† The word "stupa" refers to a sepulchral monument, a burial place or receptacle of religious objects. Stupa is the Hindu or Sanskrit name, while chorten is the Tibetan name. Originally, eight stupas were said to hold Buddha's remains divided among them, but the Emperor Ashoka later erected 84,000 more stupas to which these relics were distributed.

nearby. I could not understand the words, of course, but the actions conveyed something of the story. The play's evident good humour won the full laughter and appreciation of the Ladakhi audience.

At last, overwhelmed—indeed, stupefied—I returned to Leh.

~

The essence of travel comes when one is not doing anything or seeing anything; just being a part of the people in an everyday world into which one has been temporarily invited. The street is the primary site of life, everywhere, and that is where I spent many days in Leh.

Leh's buildings, including houses, were white-washed, flat-roofed, and two-storied, with small windows latticed in earth colours, though occasionally green or orange. The homes and guest houses were surrounded by stone walls of two to four feet in height. Irrigation systems ran throughout the town, with every inch of available land given over to planting something. Small gompas and chortens, having escaped the countryside, sometimes took up rooftop sentry posts.

Leh's main street was a clutter of shops: tailors, auto repairs, chai shops, pharmacies, banks, photographers, a Phillips Radio store, and a butcher shop. The latter sported a Rockette-like string of fresh chickens, a slab of pink mutton, and a sheep's head that smiled sideways on a cutting board, eyes staring, tongue lolling, while flies paraded.

Barkers stood outside curio shops named Cheap Muhammad's and Cheap Joe's, telling passersby to "Come in, just look. Many things. Carpets, tankas, my friend," as well as fishbone statues of Buddhist monks and fantan ladies, and hand-carved red or green perfume bottles. People leaned out from the second-storey windows, drinking tea and watching. Scores of dark-dressed women, wearing Tibetan hats with their familiar ear flaps, sat hunched beside vegetable baskets, talking, talking, endlessly talking.

Moored on a side street were more chai and curio shops cum stationery shops cum candy stores and guesthouse dives that, one suspected, came complete with hot and cold running bedbugs. A theatre, lodged behind an abbreviated wall, declared the night's feature, *An Evening in Paris*, a romantic Bollywood film from 1967.

Another street led to the Tourist Office and a hotel that proudly advertised itself as having "foot-tapping" music. But mainly, the street specialized in jewellery. Tables were laid out with various wares: dorjes, balls, and leather belts with stone carvings in-sewn; bone or ivory bracelets, necklaces, earrings, and amulets; brass or bronze statues; crude silver rings and more bracelets; semi-precious stones (turquoise, jade, emerald, opal, moonstone, lapis, and coral); jade-topped wooden boxes with white metal settings; serving-bowl human skulls, gilded in tin, and thigh bones; papier-mâché masks and boxes; wooden bowls and stone pipes (refugees from Pondicherry); and decorated conch shells.

Yet another street specialized in clothing, toiletries, and incidentals: sweaters, scarves, jeans, shirts, shawls, shoes, and shoe polish; toothpaste, soap, and cigarettes; and card games and dice. The street was the store, the open sky its ceiling. Beyond the market areas and on every street, gutters carried and often overflowed with an ensemble of detritus: Gold Flake and Panama cigarettes, Amul wrappers, and newspapers, but especially shit—dog shit, donkey shit, cow shit, horse shit—and urine, to which a few men crouched in alleys added. Dark water flowed out over the cracked pavement or drained into potholes, the contents blasted upward by the wheels of passing cars, trucks, and jeeps, horns blaring, their rusting frames bending as they turned corners. In the street, children played soccer, young men and women walked hand in hand, and old men, some with missing limbs and scarred faces, and old women, wrinkled by poverty, age, and sun, went about their day.

~

The last day of Ramadan in 1983 fell on July 10. In celebration, my Muslim landlords invited all the houseguests for tea, biscuits, and a variety of Indian/Tibetan snacks. The tearoom was in a spacious room on the hotel's upper storey, into which an abundance of windows welcomed light. We sat on Tibetan rugs before small tables. A teak cabinet stood flush against one wall, displaying pots, pans, and cutlery of both good quality and design. The family, an extended one with many children, wore their finest clothes. The older children served us, their hands bathed in henna, while also taking part in the celebration of Ramadan's end.

When not so specially welcomed, I spent my days exploring Leh's front and back streets, visiting shops, reading, watching, and listening. The majority Tibetan/Ladakhi people are physically distinct, shorter and stockier—more Mongolian—than the leaner Kashmiris. These differences similarly divided the town's cultural and social makeup. Whereas the latter generally ran the souvenir shops, the Ladakhis owned most of the guest houses and were street sellers to the few tourists. And where the Kashmiris often came across as unctuous salesmen, the Ladakhis seemed generally more friendly, warm, and smiling—more authentic.

In town, Ladakhi women generally wore long dresses in primary colours with a preference for dark blue, along with rainbow headgear and scarves, while men wore basic clothes of brown, blue, or grey. Among the mountain people, the range of colour was less: black for women, khaki or brown for men. Children were always neatly dressed, particularly on school days.

Buddhist religion, a lived reality, was much in evidence. The local cemetery was strung with flags whose inscribed prayers were meant to accompany the deceased to his or her rest; similar flags also waved like small sails throughout the immediate countryside. Believers walked holding hand-sized prayer wheels, miniature versions of the larger barrels found in temples, by which to increase the intensity of their spoken words, or played with prayer beads, an act not dissimilar to Greek worry beads or Catholic rosaries.

Ladakh borders Communist China and is thus a site of low-intensity conflict, signalled by the omnipresence of troop carriers. An Indian government pamphlet provided a helpful list of "Phrases and Words of the Ladakhi Language," including "Chinese are very bad" and "Chinese destroy gompas."

Leh sported few trustworthy restaurants or, stated another way, possessed a large number of eateries where one could reasonably expect to get food poisoning. But eating is a necessity, and so, chances must be taken. I usually ate breakfast at either the Om or the Yak Tail restaurants, the former famous for its oatmeal porridge and the latter for its Tibetan rye bread. My evening meals were at either the Om or the Dreamland. The latter was a poor hotel, but its restaurant was favoured by Westerners for its excellent meals, which were served by warm, efficient people in a comfortable atmosphere. Wherever I ate, however, there was always a gap between what the menu stated and what was available. One evening, after several agonizing minutes of decision-making, my final order came down to two types of either chow mien or chop suey; there was no chicken, no mutton, no potatoes—in fact, not much of anything else. Still, of all the meals I have eaten anywhere in the world, nothing tasted better. Eating is not just about taste; it is also about atmosphere. Just as hotdogs and beans, cooked over an open fire in a campground, seems like haute cuisine (well, almost), chicken-fried rice or a greasy omelette, when eaten in Asia, can seem like sumptuous dining.

~

I suffered one day to exchange traveller's cheques at Leh's lone bank. It was guarded nonchalantly by Indian soldiers. A sign more authoritatively proclaimed, "No weapons allowed in the bank." I had no difficulty in surmounting this restriction and quickly entered.

The next two hours were filled with endless deliberations among officials and a kind of magical performance by which my passport disappeared—a sleight-of-hand of several minutes, lateralled as if it were a rugby ball throughout the building—then suddenly reappeared, along with my requested money.

I travelled one day to the nearby village of Phyang. It was the second day of the Hemis festival, one of Ladakh's most important Buddhist festivals. It marks the birth of Guru Padmasambhava, said to have been the incarnation of Lord Buddha. Guru Padmasambhava is revered as having driven out an evil demon from Ladakh in the eight century and protected its people and culture.

The town was crowded in anticipation of the yearly celebration. A local liquor, Chhang, was on hand, and exhibits of various handicrafts were on display. Many of the townsfolk gathered around the village square to see a cluster of vibrantly dressed lamas and monks in long gowns, wearing ornate masks and other headgear.

The performers formed a circle and began what is known as the "Chham Dance," to the sound of rhythmic drumming. At the centre of the circle was a figure confined to a table around whom the performers danced, first in one direction and then the other, for several minutes. The drumming became louder and more insistent. The ceremony's purpose soon became clear: it depicted a battle between good over evil. The figure in the centre of the circle was the embodiment and the receptacle of everything evil, surrounded now by the forces of good. Suddenly, the drumming stopped. Slowly, the circle's members closed in, the scene ending with a ritual stabbing of the lone figure. Evil had been vanquished.

Evenings in Leh were a fount of various entertainments put on, not for the tourists, of whom there were few, but for and by the Ladakhi community. Each show began with a playing of the Tibetan national anthem. One evening, I listened to an ensemble of Ladakhi, Tibetan, and Hindi music by adult performers while children from a nearby refugee camp danced.* The show's venue, close to the polo field, was a small theatre constructed of pine wood with white, pasteboard walls. The metal, fold-up seats, of the type common to gymnasiums everywhere, were covered with cloth, often ripped and empty of stuffing. The stage curtains, equally torn, were of red and purple velour. A flurry of hands emerged at the end of each performance to pull the curtains together, then furtively disappeared again before returning to welcome the next act.

The next evening, in the same building, I took in a show of a very different sort. Someone had acquired a VHS tape of the Brooke Shields movie *Blue Lagoon*. A handful of other Westerners and myself, surrounded by a host of uncomprehending Ladakhis, watched the movie in complete silence. We left the venue in similar silence amid a seemingly unbridgeable cultural divide, exiting into the gathering darkness.

Ladakh's night skies are generally a vast cupola of light. Inside the city, however, nighttime came early. Even by the moon's light, its streets remained tar black, making walking at night a risky venture. The danger was compounded by a temperamental electrical system that often failed, forcing residents to rely on candles and coal oil lamps. Leh's pavements were uneven, sometimes opening up into deep, gaping holes that appeared suddenly as black blotches. Only the gurgle and gush of

---

* Days earlier, I visited the camp nine kilometres away. It housed roughly two thousand people in a series of one-story rectangular dormitories with long verandas attached.

water sometimes forewarned of the dangers ahead. A hostile beam of light from passing jeeps and trucks might temporarily blind one, then darkness again. All the while, the city's many dogs howled counterpoint to the ominous silence.

~

Inspired by sketches in a guidebook of Ladakh's monasteries and castles, I set about a few days later walking the dust-strewn streets and hills of Leh. Sitting on rocks between the squatting stupas, I pulled out my notepad and began sketching, in the end making pencil drawings of the temple of Namgyal Tsemo and two chortens.

This activity never failed to attract a crowd of admirers, mainly children—young girls in long, bright dresses and head-scarves and boys in drab grey trousers—not yet skilled in the advanced ways of art criticism.

Later that same evening, I walked to the Sankar monastery along the well-irrigated wheatfields, the high stone walls, and tiny waterfalls. The road, running along the foot of the palatial mountain, passed by a profusion of more chortens and nameless but scenic ruins and old white buildings in the Ladakhi style. I turned back finally in quest of seeing the delicate sunset coursing over the mountains.

~

*M*y days in Ladakh at last came to an end. A decidedly un-meditative impatience drove me to take a return bus to Srinagar. The ride, as always, was a new adventure. The bus's seats were narrowly divided by wooden armrests, the effect of which was to replicate what I imagine is the posture demanded by electric chairs, stiff and upright, arms stapled to the armrests. At every bump of the vehicle, my forearms and elbows were bashed hard against the wooden rests.

The bus was crowded with tired passengers. Within minutes of departure, a chorus arose of coughs, hacks, and burps preparatory to sleep. Across the aisle, a large Indian soldier on leave drowsed, his liquid weight falling heavily onto a much smaller passenger sitting beside him. The latter, his annoyance facially expressed, made repeated but subtle shrugs of his shoulder in hopes of waking his tormentor.

The bus motored on, stopping overnight again at Kargil. As before, I got a dormitory cot. As before, another inhabitant lay mummified nearby beneath a swaddle of blankets.

We set off again early the next morning and arrived later that day in Srinagar, where, for the next week, I again rented a boat on historic Lake Dal.

SRINIGAR AND THE
HMS KIPLING

L ake Dal is a historic feature of the city of Srinagar, the capital of Jammu and Kashmir. It is both a cultural and tourist attraction. Travelling to Srinigar and staying on a houseboat on Lake Dal became a thing to do for Westerners who journeyed the so-called Hippie Trail during the 1960s and 1970s. For a few Indian rupees, tourists could enjoy staying aboard such elegantly named boats as the *New Taj Mahal*, the *New Mogul*, and the *Mazda*, or, alternatively, go Western aboard the *Robin Hood* or *Alice's Restaurant*. The lake also featured a group of small, isolated islands housing old, elaborate, shuttered, and balconied hotels, such as the Hotel Heaven Canal.

When I went there in 1983, however, Lake Dal was already a victim of its own success: too many tourists, too many boats, and not enough water flow to handle the growing waste. A recent report by the International Institute for Sustainable Development* notes that "water extraction, water pollution, solid waste pollution, runoff from fertilizer use, and encroachment on the

---

*   A. M. Bassi, O. Perera, L. Wuennenberg, and G. Pallaske, *Lake Dal in Srinigar, India* (Winnipeg: International Institute for Sustainable Development, 2018). https://www.iisd.org/sites/default/files/publications/savi-dal-lake-india.pdf

lake have exceeded its carrying capacity," with the result that the lake is shrinking in size. Plans were already underway in 1983 to evacuate Dal Lake of all boats two years thence, with sections of the lake to be emptied to make way for a road.

Houseboats seemed a convenient place to stay, either for a long holiday or a short stopover. They came in four classes, A to D (A being the best), and were further classified as either Deluxe or Super Deluxe. They were priced and appointed accordingly, from the drab and dirty D models, replete with loose boards, broken windows, torn curtains, and fouled mattresses and sheets, to the more elegant Victorian A models with teak and walnut furnishings, Persian carpets, and television and stereo systems.

I had stayed briefly on a much smaller Class C houseboat (seventy feet by twelve feet) on my earlier travel through Srinigar, the owner of which was the aforementioned Rakesh. That boat featured a dining area arrayed with walnut "ball and claw" furniture, including lampstands, and three bedrooms of about equal size. My room held a double bed with a heavy but sullied mattress, three soiled pillows, two nightstands, and one plain dresser. Turning on the light switch required blindly tracing with one's fingers the open electrical wiring along the room's cross beams. Doors and windows adjoined the room's both sides. A squatter toilet, sink, and rusted tub occupied the boat's rear.

On my return journey, I opted to stay on a much larger and more exotic houseboat.

My new vessel was the *Kipling*. Made from solid pine, it was twenty-five years old and roughly 110 feet by twelve feet in size. It was primarily white in colour, with a green bottom and trim. It cost 40 rupees per day (plus tax), meals extra.

I was taken out to the *Kipling* on a shikara—a kind of boat taxi, not unlike a gondola, that ferried tourists, local salesmen, and boat owners between the boats and shore. I walked up the shikara's gangway, located at the prow, to the *Kipling*'s bow. I passed between carved wooden railings of Moghul design, just beyond which sat a couple of chairs looking out on hundreds more houseboats. Draped upon a rafter overhead was a drab white-and-green-flecked sheet, shelter against the sun. Several potted plants drearily greeted me.

A doorway led to a front room, approximately twenty-four feet by twelve feet. The room was appointed with a sofa, three large chairs, and two smaller ones, all of walnut with pink upholstery in black, regal design. In a corner stood an accountant's rolltop desk with a telephone, a pen set, and books locked—as were so many things, I quickly discovered—behind glass. Present were a vast array of tables of different types—large and small, round, oval, and square, stand-alone and nesting—nearly all of Kashmiri design. There were numerous lamps, both floor and table. Ashtrays were in abundance.

Some tables sported plastic plants, while others were laden with old books (Sidney Horler's 1939 thriller, *Here Is an SOS*, J. Edwin Orr's 1935 religious text, *The Promise is to You*, and P. G. Wodehouse's 1938 *The Code of the Woosters**). There were also several magazines (*Film World, India Today, TIME*). A Comer radio sat on another table. A cabinet's sliding doors opened up to a Telerad television, on which I one night watched *I Love Lucy*.

The walls hosted pictures of mountains and lakes, not all of India, and pale blue curtains with paisley red filigree swirls. A half-length mirror dominated the wall opposite the entrance. It was framed by carved wooden elephants and notched to hold brass goblets and candlesticks. A large Namda rug of common Kashmiri design covered the floor. The room's ceiling featured more wooden carvings, this time of elegant geometric figures whose beauty was marred only by a graceless chandelier.

Despite everything, the room did not feel cluttered. It did, however, exude the redolent must of the old Raj. To sit in one of

---

* Wodehouse's writing apparently still holds a special appeal for some Indian readers; see Vincent Dowd, "PG Wodehouse: Why India still holds a flame for the English author." BBC News, November 27, 2020. https://www.bbc.com/news/entertainment-arts-55043717

the walnut armchairs long enough seemed certain to cause the visit of a ghostly Colonel Blimp; to explore its hidden reaches, to invite a possible stumble upon some mummified corpse.

The adjoining dining room featured in the middle a commensurately carved, beautiful walnut table draped in a green vinyl tablecloth and six matching, wicker-backed chairs in place. A blue chintz light fixture hung from the ceiling.

A walnut bureau ornamented with Kashmiri dragons guarded one wall. Opposite, an enormous, teak China cabinet stood side by side with a smaller companion piece. From behind glass, a menage of China, bone-handled cutlery, papier-mâché figurines, glass and silver ware, bowls, teapots, bells, and assorted other knick-knacks looked out but were beyond touch, dutifully locked up. Two imitation velvet prayer rugs occupied other wall space, along with pictures of panoramic nature scenes similar to those found in the main room. A Namda rug again covered the floor.

Beyond the dining room were two exits. The one on the right led to a set of uneven stairs to the top balcony and a weathered roof. The latter sported a rickety table and a wind-raked clothesline. The exit on the left led first to a sink and a counter where tea was sometimes prepared for guests, then on to three eighteen-by-twelve-foot identical bedrooms that opened with a sliding door. Each bedroom had two single beds, a night table, a cushion chair, and a battered dresser with a full-length mirror and plastic flowers. White curtains bearing floral designs covered a single window. Each room had a wall lamp. Displayed on my room's wall was a calendar featuring an attractive Indian girl standing beside a bicycle. It was bracketed by two small pictures of rural scenes.

Adjoining each bedroom was a twelve-by-six-foot bathroom that, again, opened with a sliding door. The bathroom had a small sink and a very deep, boat-shaped bathtub. An elegant wood cover topped the toilet, above which was mounted a flush tank. A pull of a rope shot buckets of water into the hole, followed by the sound of a splash into the lake below.

~

wo days into my stay on the *Kipling*, I became restless; more, I felt trapped, as though stuck on a Hollywood movie set or perhaps within a small floating fish bowl. Encircling the barque was a swath of ravenous salesmen on shikaris who endlessly shouted, "Choc-o-late, cig-ar-ettes, postcards, beer! Papier-mâché, jewellery, carpets, garments!"

A thickening soup of human waste, duckweed, water ferns, and algae gathered around the houseboat. It was monsoon season, and though Lake Dal's still waters emitted a pungent odour at the best of times, the hostile fragrance now rode the moist heat to new heights of olfactory offence.

My discomfort was not the owner's fault, nor could it be blamed on his family, who resided in a tiny boat alongside the *Kipling*. Each morning for breakfast, and later for lunch and supper, I was brought food—good food—washed down with tea, politeness, and a conspicuous, though not uncomfortable, silence born of a linguistic divide; though the owner did on one occasion make some unsubtle inquiries about a female visitor who had come aboard one afternoon. No, my unease was simply that of being a human curio alone on a boat laden with pre-Mountbatten nostalgia.

Escape became increasingly necessary, so between meals, I began daily taking shikaras into the city to walk one of Srinigar's eight "wards," each of which is protected by a different deity. The city's immediate streets, where I disembarked, were straddled on either side by emporiums, cafes, fruit stands, and rent-a-bike stalls that teemed with tourists—Westerners and Indians alike.

Farther south and west were Srinagar's polo grounds, a golf course, and soccer fields, while farther west again, a strand of bridges rose, topped with more commonplace, sometimes seedier, shops. At intersections, khakied police officers wearing red sashes and turbans did a slow balletic pantomime, pretending to direct traffic while cars, trucks, and auto rick-shaws sped by, indifferent. On the streets, children swarmed about, incessantly asking, "Shikara, shikara, you want shikara?" while cocky young men in blue jeans offered to sell hashish. Completing the scene, young women in sarees huddled together, middle-aged men rubbed their pot bellies while drinking chai, and old men ran their fingers through their long beards.

Encounters with people are the chief joy of travel. The occasion need not be outsized; everyday events are often the most poignant and interesting. One day, I watched as two local women battled verbally. I didn't need to understand Hindi to realize that the point of dispute was one woman's character. The shouting grew intense, the gestures threatening. But as one woman was holding a child close in her arms and the other stood behind a phalanx of other women, the conflict stopped short of going nuclear, and each saved face.

On another occasion, I entered a pharmacy, where I asked the proprietor if he had Tiger Balm. (My shoulder was a little sore.) He didn't seem to understand, so I repeated the name. "Tiger Balm."

"Yes, yes," he said, happy that he could be helpful. He pointed at something in front of the counter but I saw nothing resembling the ointment I sought.

"Tiger Balm," I said again, this time very slowly and precisely and probably because, as humans, we tend to do this, louder.

"Yes, bomb," he said.

"No, Tiger Balm."

"Tiger bomb?"

"Tiger Balm!"

His face turned quizzical, but still trying ever so much to be helpful, he picked up a huge rocket used for fireworks displays and proudly held it out to me. "Bomb?"

I turned away, laughing. My search for Tiger Balm would have to wait.

~

On another day, I walked along Lake Nagin Road toward the Hari Parbat Fort. The fort, the last one standing in Jammu and Kashmir, rose on a hill ahead of me, but my attention was drawn to a cemetery at the foot of Sharika Hill, where lie the ruins of an earlier fort built by Akbar.

A warm and gentle rain was falling. The clouds, though everywhere bluish grey, were moving quickly. I descended to the cemetery. The place was absent headstones, but a few, low, flat, and monotonous, clung to the shallow mounds they marked. The cemetery's primary purpose was to be a pasture whose living occupants, stray cattle and marauding sheep, were chewing the grass down to mere stubble.

Seeking shelter from the drizzle, I sat under a chinar tree. A woman in Kashmiri dress came by, holding a basket from which she fed bread to the gathering pigeons, crows, and kingfishers. On a nearby grave, a part-Labrador dog lay sleeping.

The rain began to subside. I waited a while longer, then rose to leave. At that moment, another dog appeared, dragging the sun-bleached entrails of some animal. The kill was not fresh; the intestines had the rubbery look of a body in early bloat. Farther away, two more dogs hungrily gnawed the ripped underbelly of a dead sheep, their teeth bared, eyes wary, protective of their prey.

Similarly cautious, I slipped out of the cemetery to return to the houseboat.

~

Not all encounters when travelling, whether with locals or other travellers, are comfortable—just as local people can undoubtedly tell of unpleasant experiences with foreigners. One day, on my sojourns from my houseboat, I had such an uncomfortable encounter.

My afternoon began as usual with lunch, followed by a

shikara ride into the city. It was a warm day, and I was wearing cut-off shorts and a T-shirt. Unlike previous ventures into the city, I was going this time with the specific purpose of finding a tailor, whose name I had been given, to do some minor repairs.

Upon landing, I was directed toward Lal Chowk. As I walked along a typical dusty street toward my destination, a tall Kashmiri man joined in step with me. After a time, he spoke.

"Hello, where are you going?"

"For a walk."

He mumbled my words back to himself, then: "Which country are you from?"

"Canada."

"What is your job?"

Seeking to end the interrogation, I replied, "Teacher."

He fell silent. Everything might have ended there, except that I made the fatal mistake of then asking how far it was to Lal Chowk.

"Come, I will take you there," he said, and so we set off. As the minutes passed, however, we seemed no closer to anything, even as he regularly assured me that the street, like judgment day, was at hand. Then, suddenly, "Please, will you do me a favour and send me a letter with a picture of a naked girl?"

Today, anyone with a decent—or should I say, indecent—cellphone can quickly find pornography. His request seems thus curiously innocent. At the time, however, I was taken aback and, at first, didn't understand, or perhaps didn't want to understand, what he was asking.

This made him quickly repeat his request. Until this time, he had appeared only as a shadow on my periphery. But now, stopping in the middle of the street, I turned and, for the first time, actually saw his face. His eyes were glazed but wide; his features pale and gaunt. Spittle glistened on the right side of his mouth.

He asked again and was insistent that the girl in the photo be naked. "All naked, like this," he said and, with a clammy finger, touched my exposed shoulder.

Wishing to be done with him, I told him I would.

He then made a second request. "You do me one more favour?"

I was prepared for just about anything at this point, except for what came next.

"Send me a Japanese pen."

I was again startled to silence. Sensing once more that perhaps I had not heard, he repeated his request.

"They are good pens?" I asked.

He didn't answer, instead saying, "If you like, I can take you to my cousin. You can marry her."

I knew what he meant, of course, but replied with intentional naivete that this would be unfair as I was leaving in a few days.

He had an answer for that. "You can marry her for a few hours."

"How old is she?" I asked.

"Twenty-two," adding, "she is free."

"Has she been married before?"

"No."

"How would she feel about this?"

"She will be happy because you are my friend."

I said I was not interested, but he continued to cling to me, repeatedly asking whether the women in my country were "free" and if we fucked every day.

"Not every day," I said wryly. He was unconvinced.

By now, through sheer luck, we had arrived at Lal Chowk. But how to be rid of him?

I told him to write down his address so that I could send the photo. He went to a store nearby and soon returned with the information, then walked away, his parting words, "Don't forget the pen."

I returned to my houseboat. Four days later, I left the *Kipling* for the last time to begin my journey to Dharamshala.

DALHOUSIE, DHARAMSHALA, AND MCLEOD GANJ

The distance from Srinagar to Dharamshala is only 465 kilometres, but it takes nearly nine hours by road. The first leg of my journey thus took me to Jammu, where my bus arrived five hours later. It was 8 p.m.

I quickly got a top-floor hotel room for fifteen rupees. My room overlooked a mosque and market street. The evening sky was a wondrous blend of pale blues and pinks, broken up by translucent clouds.

It was monsoon season, a period announced every year in Jammu by the arrival of tens of thousands of gnats (a.k.a. midges). Usually, the beasts congregate in large empty fields or above streets, but on this occasion, they set up headquarters in my room. Fortunately, however, my room also came equipped with a small grey lizard. I wondered: was the lizard an extra service, like fresh water, a fan, or a television, provided to premium guests? ("Your room comes with its own lizard.") But if this was the case, the perquisite failed, as the lizard was soon overwhelmed by the swarm of invading insects.

No matter. Greatly fatigued, I hid under the sheets, sleeping well through the night, woken only by the pummelling onset of rains and a bout of diarrhea brought on (I suspected) by a mutton dish earlier in the day. Dodging the gnats in the sink, I washed up and went to the bus station, where I caught a noon bus first to Pathankot (two hours) and then on to Dalhousie (two and a half hours).

The journey to Pathankot took place amid heavy monsoon rains that, within minutes, turned otherwise dry ravines and highways into rivers and rendered gutters and roads indistinguishable. Heedless of danger or discomfort, our bus driver nonetheless plowed ahead through ditch and pothole, sending frequent geysers of brackish water halfway up the bus windows. The other passengers and I bounced high above our seats, briefly defying gravity before crashing down. I felt as though I were riding a mechanical bull.

Thankfully, the rains lifted on the forward journey to Dalhousie. A green lustre replaced the grey hills, and a lush fragrance escaped the moist ferns and pine trees. As if celebrating the rain's short respite, monkeys flitted about the roadways between the wandering cows and oxen.

I arrived at last in Dalhousie. The town of a few thousand people was established in the late nineteenth century as a hill station in the northern Indian state of Himachal Pradesh. It was one of several cantonments built after the Sepoy uprising in 1857 to quarter British troops. It is named after Lord Dalhousie, India's Governor-General, whose time in office coincided with the introduction of railways, the telegraph, and uniform postage, but also the uprising.

On the main square above the bus depot stands the Catholic Church of St. Francis, built in 1894 by the Army and Civil Officers and civilians, and nearby, the priests' residence, the Alverna. Outside the church, a series of signs in English, with Hindi translation, proclaim the happiness that the poor, the pure, the meek, and the merciful might obtain in the hereafter.

Beyond the walls of St. Francis, a plethora of schools beckoned: St. Anthony's Nursery (Hindi Medium), Holy Heart School (English Medium), the Himgiri School ("Run on Rudolf

Steiner's Pattern of Education"*), the Himalaya Academy of Self-Culture, operating out of the Snow View Hotel, and others. The town was also well-resourced with government services (postal, police, and hospital), private clinics, the St. Joseph's Nursing Home, run by the Sisters of Charity, and a host of very Western-named clubs: the Lions, the Rotary, and the Dalhousie Club, the latter a green bungalow affair near the bus stand that overlooked the valley.

Especially prominent were signs promoting the "famous and magnificent" Aroma-N-Claire Hotel. The hotel, along Court Road, stood beside the nursing home, its presence announced in no uncertain terms by an even larger sign: "This Is the Famous Hotel Aroma-N-Claire," followed apologetically by, "This is the front side. Back is exquisite."

The hotel's Victorian lobby was indeed exquisite. If so inclined, a tourist could purchase a small paperweight statue of the Eiffel Tower or the Greek Parthenon.

The Aroma-N-Claire was not singular in its English ambience. Like the houseboat I had earlier rented on Dal Lake, much of the town, its hotels and street names, exuded nostalgia for the British Raj. Side by side with the swarm of Indian residents and tourists, one sensed the invisible presence of tall khakied *bwana sahibs* with handlebar moustaches that covered stiff upper lips, who wore pith helmets and carried swagger sticks.

I walked along a side street leading to the town's lower residential quarter. The buildings there evinced the picturesque squalor of an English factory town. The strains of "Clementine" could be heard from a tea stall.

The valley below the town was beautiful by morning light. By late morn, however, the monsoon clouds moved in. The valley took on the appearance of damp smoke until becoming obscured altogether, save for islands of mossy trees that lifted their heads in floating patches above the mist.

------

* https://en.wikipedia.org/wiki/Rudolf_Steiner

I made a short journey to the nearby village of Chamba—"Population: 24 souls"—to take in a fair, but left the next day by bus. The trip was long and tedious, what is referred to in North America as "the milk run." The bus churned up relentlessly rising and winding hills, stopping frequently to let passengers get off or get on or, due to the narrowness of roads, to back up and let oncoming traffic pass. Below us were terraced hills of cultivated rice paddies, bungalows, and peasant farmers. A huge water buffalo was wallowing in mud.

A heavy mugginess hung over the day. As more passengers got on and few left, the bus soon became standing-room only. The bus became a mobile sauna. Our forty-some bodies comingled in the production of oily sweat. Water ran down my face and settled on my hands and under my fingernails. I smelled myself, and it was not good, but there was no escape. The window latches, being rusted, did not open. A choking stench set in. Finally, a man in front of me pried open his window. A faint but welcome breeze blew in. At last, a few passengers disembarked—relief.

The hours passed. My ass grew numb from sitting; my legs were gimped. As if in the opening line of a joke, a drummer, a trumpeter, and a clarinetist got on the bus. But the drummer played in syncopation without form, the trumpeter in mock imitation of jamming, and the clarinetist in accordance with his personal vision of New Orleans jazz. What they lacked in talent, however, they made up for in enthusiasm and volume. The trapped audience seemed to enjoy the musicians, who departed an hour later with a box brimming with rupees.

~

Eight hours after my journey began, I arrived in Dharamshala. It was 5 p.m. when I took yet another bus, thankfully a short trip, to the suburb of McLeod Ganj, also known as "Little Lhasa," where the Dalai Lama and the Tibetan government-in-exile reside. I got a room for the night at the Rainbow Guest House and Restaurant and, after eating a feast of Tibetan food, settled down for the evening, reading a Hemingway novel.

I moved the next day to the less-expensive Himalayan Hotel and Restaurant. My double room cost 14 rupees per night. It had two basic beds and a table. There was shelving along one of the blue-and-green-washed walls and windows that opened onto the misted valley below.

The hotel's toilets were on the roof. The stairway to the roof was not lit, so navigating the steps at night required memory and intuition, in part to avoid a vacant doghouse and a clothesline strung lethally at neck level.

By day, the streets below echoed with the sounds of construction men chiselling and breaking stone and the seasonal gagging of water running in ditches. In the evenings, rain tap-tapped on the corrugated tin roofs of nearby houses. I sometimes sat on my room's window ledge, looking out, the eaves protecting me from the rain, lights off so as not to attract moths, flies, and mosquitoes. The only truly discordant note at night was the lunatic howling and fighting of innumerable dogs. On the streets each morning, giant flying cockroaches lay belly-up, done in by the heat, the rain, and their own obesity.

I quickly learned that religious prayer was an ever-present part of daily life. Chants of "Om" greeted me everywhere. I entered a small shop whose owner was sitting behind his glass display case, chanting loudly and repeatedly.

"This jar is twelve rupees?" I asked.

"Om—yes—Om," he replied.

I pointed to a small red cylinder in the case. "Is that Tiger Balm?" (I had not given up my search.)

"Om—yes, Tiger Balm—Om."

"How much is it?"

"Om—three rupees—Om."

I paid him and said, "Thanks," but there was no answer, only the low drone of "Om" as I left the store.

~

McLeod Ganj is a fairly dispersed district. Its focal point is the main square where buses arrive, from which a series of routes meander, Medusa-like. To begin in any direction might mean very quickly going in another direction. Within minutes, for example, the immediate route heading north branched into one road travelling northwest to Dal Lake*, while another headed to the hill station of Triund, nine kilometres to the southeast. My time in MacLeod Ganj was spent walking three other primary routes, which, though similar, contained quite distinct interests.

The first primary route, southwest, leads to Dharamshala. Two kilometres along the road, idyllically situated between the pines, is the Church of St. John in the Wilderness, a typical English church in much need of repair. It is the final resting place of Lord Elgin, who—before becoming Viceroy and Governor-General of India, where he died in 1863—was Governor-General of the (then) Province of Canada. Besides Elgin, the Christian cemetery features several headstones that read like short and tragic novelettes: an apothecary of the Hussars, dead at thirty-three; a lieutenant and his three children, all deceased between July 6 and 13, 1875, of an epidemic, perhaps cholera; and a number of people killed in an earthquake in April 1905. Between these marked graves, a spat of numbered metal plates, overgrown with moss and indistinct from each other, lay stapled to the earth.

The second primary route, while ostensibly heading southeast, soon birthed four smaller paths. One of these quickly descended toward the Om Hotel and Restaurant and then into

---

* Though of the same name, this Dal Lake is not the same one as in Srinigar.

the valley. Another passed the Friendly Café, a series of curio shops and other restaurants occupying two-storey buildings.

The street's left side was dominated by a large, gold-topped chorten, next to which sat a gompa, and further on, fruit stalls, restaurants, and a touristy hotel located on a hillock. But the chorten and gompa were the centrepiece, around which Westerners and locals gathered throughout the day to sell their wares: shirts, sweaters, scarves, jeans, rings, carpets, saddle blankets, hats, used books, etcetera. Westerners sat there every evening, chanting and singing songs.

The final, more intriguing, path began in front of the Tashin Tibetan Restaurant. The restaurant had bamboo walls, Western music, an owner who really liked Golden Eagle beer, and a clientele consisting mainly of Western freaks and local alcoholics. While eschewing membership in either of these groups, I nonetheless ate there on a couple of occasions as the food was both good and cheap.

Beyond the Tashin Tibetan Restaurant were a brace of fruit stands, curio shops, and restaurants, including the Tibet Memory Restaurant. After this, one came to a series of carpet factories, where the clang and bang of work continued throughout the long day, six days a week. An army of women sat on shop floors or on low seats in front of hand looms while men cut and snipped threads of carpet in preparation. The work, for which all earned a pittance, was onerous; a situation sadly little changed today."

The road thereafter was steep. By day, it glistened damp diamonds and spun a thin fog, out of which a variegated parade of people and animals might suddenly emerge: ambling water buffaloes, fiery-headed roosters and docile cows, and Tibetans holding mushroom-like umbrellas. They were joined by red- and purple-garbed monks, youthful, bald, and smiling, their shawls slung over their shoulders. Curbside, small children stirred the puddles with sticks or squatted to urinate.

Passing the Tibetan Library, the route at last came to a small teashop, about twelve feet by twelve feet, furnished with a few tables, benches, a coal oil stove, a clay pot in one corner, and empty pop bottles. Boxes of glucose biscuits, coconut cookies, buns, and shortbread rested on an overworked counter. A shelf held a glass container of candies. A basket of eggs hung from the ceiling in one corner. Two small windows looked out on the foggy valley.

The shop owner was a man, short and slight of build, whose concave face was narrowed even more by an absence of teeth. His tanned skin stood out against a white shirt and brown pants. The walls behind him were proudly ecumenical, featuring a Guru Narak calendar, a picture of Christ, a statue of Buddha, a picture of Shiva, and a photo of the Dalai Lama. An array of signs read, "It is nice to be important, but it is more important to be nice," "Truth is Immortal," and "Peace is Mankind's."

The third primary route, tacking northeast, began where the aforementioned Rainbow Guest House stood. As elsewhere, the route proceeded along an avenue of curio shops, food stalls, and hotels: the stylish Hotel Tibet on the right, the less than stylish Nyana Hotel on the left, followed by the goldilocks Koko Nor Tibetan Hotel and Restaurant, flanked by the Security and Pass-port Office and the Tibetan Medical Institute.

The road split thereafter, the right-hand side descending into a wide valley, while the narrow left-hand path led past my quar-ters in the Himalayan Hotel, then high above a pine- and fir-tree-lined valley whose slopes evinced a fuzzy, swaddling warmth. I passed bungalow-style houses, squatted on the far hills and, after a time, crossed a bridge spanning a gurgling stream; then, a little farther on, the Lovely Guest House, a green building with a front veranda that featured a friendly patron. Just ahead were more small hotels and tiny shops until finally, I came to the Bhagsunath Rock Garden and, soon, a faded-red archway leading to its famous temple, where I was greeted by competing chai shops.

I stopped for a plate of breaded onion bits and a milk tea, 1.5

rupees. Above the archway, a plaque informed me it had been erected in memory of the Gurkha Rifles, who had quartered in the area in 1864-65.

A set of stairs led upward inside the temple to a bell hung from a low ceiling, the latter festooned with mythical Hindu figures and photos of monks. Nearby, a holy man was giving council to his followers. I moved about quietly so as not to disturb them.

Below this room, a solitary waiting area beckoned, with a mountain-fed holy pool. Children were bathing and frolicking in the cool, fresh water. (The water is considered holy and believed to have legendary properties; it is a civil offence to drink it.)

A crippled man sat in the waiting room, smoking a cigarette, oblivious to my presence.

Close by, a wretchedly disfigured individual, his eyes and gnarled teeth chaotically arranged, clung to the shadows. Another maimed individual was being carried by his companion to the healing waters.

I was reminded of a scene I had witnessed only days before on a street in MacLeod Ganj. A short, stocky man dressed in workman's dungarees was carrying a large, rolled bundle of bedding when suddenly he crashed to the muddy pavement as though grabbed by an unseen hand. His torso stiffened. His legs rotated upwards and inwards while his hands jangled erratically in front of him as though frantically chasing away flies. The poor man's eyeballs rolled like escaping pinballs, and his lips drooped. He was having a seizure. It was a painful sight to behold.

Two men had then cautiously brought the afflicted man to a kneeling position while a third sprayed water into his gaping mouth. One of the first men used a cloth to wipe the snot from the seized man's contorted face. He said nothing; at that moment, he had no say over his own life. Slowly, his benefactors took him by his still-twitching legs and arms and lifted him away from the road, where a concerned woman chided them not to put him near some bristles. Someone else retrieved the man's bundle and placed it against a wall for him to lean on. Another individual placed his sandals nearby. There seemed nothing to do but wait for the seizure to pass.

~

Travel takes you to places in yourself you might not otherwise visit because of the presence of others. Each journey is augmented by newness. My too-brief time in India in 1983 was stimulated by new sights, sounds, and smells, but also by an array of books that ranged from history, philosophy, religion, and political theory to fiction; by day, in cafes, chai shops, or the McLeod Ganj library, or at night in my room, bathed in solitude. When not reading, I spent my time drawing sketches, writing notes, or making outlines for short stories.

A final tale of that time. I made a short journey to Chandigarh, staying at a severely overpriced guest house, then on to Haridwar, and finally to Dehradun, where I obtained similarly overpriced accommodation, though the room did include a bath and toilet. I went for a good meal at a local vegetarian restaurant, then to the bus station.

The station had a weigh scale costing ten paise. I stepped on. The machine dutifully spewed out a card stating my calculated weight. It was out by about twenty pounds. Written in both Sanskrit and English on the card's reverse side was a medium's description of my character: "You have a true comprehension of life, its difficulties and problems." Given how badly the machine had determined my weight, I was not persuaded of its characterological accuracy.

I made a brief journey to the hill station towns of Landour and Mussoorie in Uttarakhand, to visit the young woman who had weeks earlier visited me on the *HMS Kipling* on Lake Dal and now was teaching at the international Woodstock School.

But the weeks of daily travel were wearing on me, as were other thoughts of what I wanted to do with my life. I shortly thereafter took a bus to Delhi where I boarded a flight home to Canada.

While other adventures awaited me, it would be several years before I engaged again in foreign travel.

EPILOGUE

These stories conclude in 1983. In the years that followed, I got married, had two children, completed my graduate education, and began my professional career. There are other stories I could tell: the incident of an abused bidet in Paris and of not meeting the Turkish author Orhan Pamuk in Istanbul, though I did meet *both* his American cousin *and* a Persian cat named Pamuk while in the city. But who hasn't experienced such things?

Another book? Perhaps. Life is nothing if not a collection of stories.

ACKNOWLEDGMENTS

My thanks to the many people, mostly unnamed but not forgotten, who are the *dramatis personae* of these stories. Without them, there would be nothing to say.

As usual, my wife, Terri, read early and later renditions of the stories and caught several grammatical errors. A special thanks to Elizabeth McLaughlin, whose corrections, suggestions, and encouragement were invaluable in putting the collection together.

My thanks and appreciation go also to Edward Willett, who saw in his reading of an initial manuscript a book worthy of publication.

Special thanks to Colleen Bakker for permission to use her painting on the book's cover.

As always, any errors or omissions are entirely mine.

ABOUT THE AUTHOR

Trevor W. Harrison

Trevor W. Harrison is a retired Professor of Sociology at the University of Lethbridge. He is best known for his studies in political sociology, political economy, and public policy. He is the author, co-author, or co-editor of eleven books, including a book of poetry, as well as numerous journal articles, chapters, and reports. Dr. Harrison is a frequent contributor to public media, including radio and television.

Founded by award-winning author Edward Willett, Endless Sky Books assists authors with publishing all kinds of books, from children's books to poetry to novels to nonfiction. Select titles, like this one, are distributed under the Endless Sky Books imprint of Shadowpaw Press (shadowpawpress.com). Find out more at endless-sky-books.com.

www.ingramcontent.com/pod-product-compliance
Lightning Source LLC
Chambersburg PA
CBHW040907010826
48978CB00013BB/1180